*W*HEN LOVE DIES
How to Save a Hopeless Marriage

Judy Bodmer

THOMAS NELSON
Since 1798

NASHVILLE   DALLAS   MEXICO CITY   RIO DE JANEIRO

Published in Nashville, Tennessee, by Thomas Nelson. Thomas Nelson is a registered trademark of Thomas Nelson, Inc.

Thomas Nelson, Inc. titles may be purchased in bulk for educational, business, fund-raising, or sales promotional use. For information, please e-mail SpecialMarkets@ThomasNelson.com.

Unless otherwise indicated Scripture quotations used in this book are from The New International Version (NIV) © 1973, 1978, 1984 International Bible Society. Used by permission of Zondervan Bible Publishers.

Other Scripture quotations are from:

The Living Bible (TLB) © 1971 by Tyndale House Publishers, Wheaton, Ill. Used by permission.

The Message (THE MESSAGE) © 1993. Used by permission of NavPress Publishing Group.

The New King James Version (NKJV) © 1979, 1980, 1982, Thomas Nelson, Inc., Publishers.

The *Holy Bible*, New Living Translation (NLT). © 1996 by Tyndale Charitable Trust. All rights reserved. Used by permission.

The New Revised Standard Version (NRSV). © 1989, Division of Christian Education of the National Council of Churches of Christ in the USA. Used by permission.

Library of Congress Cataloging-in-Publication Data

Bodmer, Judy. 1950–
    When love dies : how to save a hopeless marriage / by Judy Bodmer.
      p.   cm.
    ISBN 978-0-8499-3714-9
    1. Marriage. 2. Marriage—Psychological aspects. 3. Love. 4. Divorce.
  5. International relations. I. Title.
    HQ734.B666 1999
    306.81—dc21   99-24421
                                                                CIP

Printed in the United States of America

13 QG 24 23 22 21 20

1. Criticism –
2. Contempt –
3. Stonewalling distancing
   to perceived criticism
4. Defensiveness

*T*his book is dedicated to my husband, Larry, whose
love and encouragement and steadfast belief in our marriage,
even during the hard years, made all of this possible.

And to my friend Jesus Christ,
who loves me just the way I am.

Contents

Contents

Acknowledgments

I owe a special thanks to my writing groups and prayer partners, Peggy King Anderson, Janet Carey, Peg Kehle, Dawn Knight, Katherine G. Bond, Jan Keller, Tammy Perron, Scott Pinzon, Thorn Ford, Johnna Howell, Paul Malm, and Lisa Foster. They kept me going when I wanted to quit. They loved me when I didn't much care for myself and taught me how to be persistent in the face of discouragement.

I also owe Kent Crockett a big thanks for helping me find my agent, Steven L. Green, who opened the door to Word.

Finally, thanks to the wonderful staff at Thomas Nelson: Joey Paul, Laura Kendall, Pamela McClure, Debbie Wickwire, and to my editor, Nancy Norris.

Introduction

*I*t has taken me fifteen years to write this book. I thought I needed a perfect marriage in order to speak to other women about improving theirs. I've realized I will never reach that goal, so I'm writing this book from my heart. I'm writing as someone who sometimes struggles with her feelings for her husband. There have been times I haven't felt much love for him; there have been times I've even wondered if I liked him. I'm speaking as someone who has come to the edge of divorce, but stayed—even though I didn't feel like it. I stayed believing that if I did the right thing, God would renew my love. Through my struggles, I've learned a thing or two, and I want to share them with you, not as an expert, but as a friend. I am imperfect, just as I suspect you are. I hope our hearts will touch at the point of our imperfections. And because of that, you'll be encouraged.

CHAPTER ONE

When Love Dies

You turned my wailing into dancing;
you removed my sackcloth and clothed me with joy.
PSALM 30:11

𝓘 was married in a small town in northern Idaho. The church was filled with my friends, my relatives, and people of the community who felt like family because I'd known them all my life. The organist played the opening chords of the "Wedding March." I took my father's arm. The stiffness around his mouth was the only sign of the struggle he was having at giving me away to a man he hardly knew. We slowly walked down the aisle together, he tall and proud, and me frightened and excited, toward my beginning and his ending.

Larry looked pale. It was hard to tell if it was from the flu he'd had the week before or from the commitment he was about to make. We exchanged our vows. They were simple words that pledged our love through better or worse, richer or poorer, in sickness and in health.

If I'd been honest that day I would have said something like this: "Larry, you've made me feel beautiful, feminine, smart, and funny. You're the first person who truly accepted me for who I am. We can talk about anything. The hours we've spent together have been pure joy. I feel fulfilled and complete. I've never experienced such happiness. And Larry, I expect you to make me feel this way for the rest of my life."

Six months later, I sat in a small apartment in Seattle, which my parents referred to as a closet, and wondered what I'd done. All my friends were in Idaho, and Larry, who only a few months before couldn't live without me, was too busy at his new job to talk to me on the phone. All I had was a black-and-white TV to keep me company. The man whom I couldn't wait to spend the rest of my life with now seemed distracted and uninterested. The fun-loving college student who took me to parties and movies and on sleigh rides suddenly had all these errands to run and chores to do. He measured the success of his days by how many things he marked off his to-do list. Resentment and dissatisfaction began growing in my heart.

Instead of dealing with it, I buried it. I didn't feel I had a right to complain, and I surely didn't want to start a fight or hurt my husband's feelings. I chose another path. I went back to school and got my degree. Tensions eased as I developed my own career, and we began to make plans for our future.

Six years later, we had a baby, a home, and two careers. We went to church every Sunday, participated in Bible studies and evangelism programs, planted flowers in the garden beds, and put on a smile for everyone who walked through our door. From the outside, it appeared we had it all. Even if you had sat at our kitchen table, you would not have known anything was amiss.

Then Larry found himself unemployed. I was frightened; he withdrew even farther. We became strangers sitting across the table from each other, and we were angry. We couldn't talk about anything without losing our tempers or getting our feelings hurt. I wanted Larry to fix what was wrong. But the more I yelled, the more he withdrew until neither of us wanted much to do with the other. We shared the same bed and even had another baby.

Two babies, a marriage that was failing, and we were Christians. A pastor told me it was a spiritual problem. Get right with God, then everything would be okay. I prayed, but it seemed as though God wasn't listening. I dreaded Sunday mornings. I hated putting on that phony smile that said to the world everything was okay, when everything wasn't okay. I withdrew from all of my church activities, avoided my Christian friends, and started overeating. Good Christians didn't have bad marriages. I felt ashamed.

I began to play with the idea of getting a divorce. Living alone had to be more honest than living this lie.

If you are where I was then, I have some good news. Divorce wasn't the answer. I found another way, and I want to share it with you. Through the chapters of this book you'll discover a way back to the love that was once yours. Your marriage doesn't have to end. This can be the beginning of learning about yourself and rediscovering the man you married. It also can be a time to begin a lifetime of happiness, not because you have all the wonderful feelings that first love offers, but because you've seen your husband at his worst, he's seen you at yours, you've accepted who you are, and you want to remain married. It's a mature love; one made of steel because it has been tested.

This book isn't for your husband.* It's for you. The things I'll discuss will be practical suggestions that have helped other women

---

* This book is designed for the 83 percent of marriages that end because of lack of commitment and immaturity of one or both partners. If you are in an abusive relationship, I strongly suggest you seek out professional help. Most police departments have advocates for abuse victims. The National Domestic Violence Hotline is 1-800-799-7233.

who've been through similar experiences and ultimately brought me the happiness that I'd been seeking. We'll explore:

- Why divorce may actually make your problems worse.

- How you can change from the inside out. Not just for a few days, but forever.

- Ways to renew your love. We'll review the normal cycle of married life, discussing what may lead to spiritual separation and finally divorce. We'll see what effect the fall of Adam and Eve has on marriage today. We'll discover that what God asks of us is exactly what will lead to our happiness.

- Some simple techniques that will draw your husband toward you instead of repelling him.

- Some simple things you and your husband can do to relight the fires of your sexual relationship.

- Adultery because you're vulnerable. And if you're thinking it could never happen to you, then you're particularly susceptible. We'll address the affairs of the mind, probably the biggest barrier to finding satisfaction with your husband.

- How to find friends and how to keep them. They cannot fulfill all your needs, just as a husband cannot, but they are an important aspect of a healthy life. Ten years ago I would have said I had no friends. Now I have several. They've helped me stay on track and have undergirded the strength of my faith and marriage.

• How you can find what you want, not in a divorce court, but in a relationship with Jesus Christ.

This book will be a journey that won't always be easy. You're going to read some things that will make you uncomfortable. But this is good. It is only when we are uncomfortable that we are motivated to change. Perhaps what you're going through is exactly what you need to find the happiness you've always wanted. Remember nothing grows on the mountaintops, but only in the valleys.

Action item: There is an assignment at the end of each chapter. You may find they will help you put into practice the principles that we're learning. Your first task is to read the next chapter.

CHAPTER TWO

It's for the Best

"I hate divorce," says the LORD, the God of Israel.
MALACHI 2:16, NRSV

I lay in bed staring at the darkness. Larry, his back to me, was snoring softly. We'd had another fight. I could hardly remember what had started it, but he'd said ugly things. His voice was full of hate. I begged him to stop, but he didn't. I responded in kind, wanting to hurt him, wanting him to put his arms around me and hold me, to make me feel better. Instead, I felt as if my belly had been cut open and I was bleeding profusely. Nothing had been resolved. We'd just gotten tired, and now he slept and I lay there alone.

I crawled out of bed to check on our small sons, Matthew and David. David, who was a handful when awake, looked like an angel. I stroked his face. It was still sticky from the ice-cream cone he'd eaten earlier.

I covered Matthew and smoothed his blond head. He needed a

haircut. Working full-time, two small sons to referee, and a house to keep clean, I never had enough time to do it all.

Something drew me to the window. There was a full moon and I could see the skyscrapers in downtown Seattle. So many people. What were they doing? Were they as lonely as I? Was there anyone out there who cared?

"God," I cried, "help me find the strength to leave."

I already knew where I wanted to live. On my way home from work, I passed a new apartment building. Red and white impatiens filled the flower beds in front and balconies overlooked a small valley. It looked peaceful.

I could get away from the pain. Yes, it would be lonely, but I had never felt as lonely as I did now.

It would be better for the boys. It wasn't good that they heard us fight. It wasn't good for them to live in a house so full of tension.

It would be better for Larry. He could find someone who loved him. He was a nice guy. He deserved someone who could appreciate him. Obviously we weren't right for each other. Our marriage had been a mistake. There was time to start over.

I knew God didn't like divorce, but I couldn't believe he wanted me to live like this for the rest of my life. No one could say I hadn't tried. I'd read the books; I'd gone for counseling; I'd spent hours crying to God, begging him to heal my marriage. It had been three years and nothing had changed; it had only grown worse.

People dissolved their marriages all the time; they seemed happy, and their children seemed to be doing fine. Divorce had to be the answer.

THE TRUTH ABOUT DIVORCE

Is this true? Are those people getting along fine? I've done some research, and I'd like to share with you some facts.

Lie #1. Divorce will be better for you.
When I was hurting, all I wanted to do was get away from the pain. The consequences seemed minor in comparison. It was like an aching tooth, all I could think about was having it pulled.

What I didn't know was that divorce would be, as my mother used to say, like jumping from the frying pan into the fire.

"Little you can do to your mind that's worse than divorce," says psychologist Diane Medved, author of *The Case against Divorce*. At first, you might feel relief, but that is short-lived. Tests show that for the first five to six years you will be consumed by moderate to severe anger. Depression, which at its very core is a feeling of failure, will become your companion. One writer called it a private hell. Stress tests rank separation and divorce as the second and third most traumatic events in a person's life. The only thing more stressful is the death of a spouse. Seventy percent of divorced women report feelings of worry and anxiety seven and eight years later. For some survey participants, these feelings lasted for twenty to thirty years.[1]

This shouldn't be surprising when you look at the Bible. In Genesis it says, "Therefore a man shall leave his father and mother and be joined to his wife, and they shall become one flesh."[2] The word used for "flesh" is the same word used to describe the attachment of muscle to bone.[3] The pain of tearing living tissue is reflected in the pain of tearing apart a relationship.

Divorce may cost you your friends. One year four of our close friends divorced. Today, I rarely see any of the wives. I didn't mean to lose them, but one left town, and two others made life choices that I couldn't support. The last one just sort of drifted out of my life. As a single she no longer fits into the couple times we'd had before.

What about finding someone new, more compatible? According to a report done in 1986, the chance of a college-educated woman over thirty getting married is 20 percent. By the age of thirty-five, the odds drop to 5 percent. An article in *Newsweek* magazine reported that "forty-year-olds are more likely to be killed by a terrorist: they have a minuscule 2.6 percent probability of tying the knot."[4]

If you have someone already in mind, you may be interested to know that 70 percent of those who divorce have an extramarital lover. However, only 15 percent actually marry that person.[5] Remember, too, that this person you're so enamored with is a home wrecker. And if he's married, his infidelity will probably repeat itself in your relationship. I saw this happen to a friend who left her husband for a married man. They married, but it wasn't long until he left her for another woman.

Even if you remarry, stepfamilies disrupt established loyalties, create new uncertainties, provoke deep anxieties, and sometimes threaten a child's physical safety as well as emotional security. The question of discipline has destroyed many second marriages. Even if the children seemingly support the new husband before the wedding, afterward things can change. Combining two families is much like playing Russian roulette. You don't know what you have until you pull the trigger. One parent confided in me that the grandparents of her husband's children were rich and showered expensive gifts on her stepchildren, while her children went without. This naturally created much resentment.

Studies also show that children in a stepfamily are more than forty times more likely to suffer sexual or physical abuse.[6] I've recently heard from two women that they've postponed remarriage until their children are out of the house, for that very reason.

You may also lose your church friends. They probably won't be as loving as you imagined. I know of a church that practices church discipline. After months of trying to get a wife to reconcile with her husband, she filed for divorce. The elders read her name from the pulpit, and the congregation was asked not to associate with her until she returned to her family. Your friends, who seem so sympathetic now, may stop calling and start avoiding you because they are uncomfortable with your decision. "Most divorced people," according to Christian pollster George Barna, "cling to their beliefs after divorce, but are more likely to drop out of organized church because they no longer feel welcomed."[7]

The saddest possible consequence is that you may lose your children. More and more judges are awarding custody to a husband, especially if the wife has a career. They believe that working mothers are too aggressive or career-oriented to properly care for their children.[8] Even if you don't physically lose them, you might lose them emotionally. One study showed that only half of the children who were close to their mothers before a divorce remained equally close to their mothers after the divorce. Boys particularly have difficulties with their mothers.[9]

Have you considered the financial side of divorce? Are you prepared to live on what you make? On the average your standard of living will go down by 73 percent. This drop in income forces many women to work more hours, get a second job, or go on welfare.[10] According to the 1991 Census Bureau, one in three single mothers lives in poverty.[11]

You may think your husband will be forced to take care of you, but in this age of no-fault divorce, alimony is rare, and if you're making more money than your husband, you may be forced to pay alimony to him. If you're planning on child support, you might be interested to know it won't cover the expense of another household.[12] Even if you're awarded child support, there's no guarantee that your husband will pay. In Canada 50 to 75 percent of fathers don't make child-support payments.[13] In the United States fewer than half of the 11.5 million single-parent families receive any money from the non-custodial parent.[14]

Did you know you might lose your home? A judge ordered one woman I know to pay her husband half of the equity in their home. Are you prepared to do that? Statistics show that most women are forced to move within the first year of their divorce for financial reasons.[15]

Even if you aren't forced to sell your house in the divorce settlement, you may be forced to sell it to pay off your lawyer's fees. The average divorce can run $5,000–$30,000.[16] A woman I know just spent $5,000 trying to get more child support from her husband so her daughter could go to college.

I know you can't imagine ever regretting your decision, but you probably will. Removing a painful tooth seems like a good answer. The truth is, there are hidden consequences. I have a friend who makes dentures for a living. He told me that the extraction of a tooth could lead to the ones surrounding it loosening. In the long run, you may lose all of your teeth. Pulling a tooth is a temporary solution that may lead to greater problems, just like divorce.

Lie #2. It will be better for your children.
When I was growing up, I knew one child of divorce. She was small for her age, her clothes were either too large or too small, and often she would come to school dirty, her hair uncombed. She didn't do well in school and had few friends. She wasn't allowed to belong to Camp Fire Girls or our church youth group, play sports, or join any other after-school activity. She had to run home and help take care of her little sisters and cook dinner. In high school she had a reputation, became pregnant out of wedlock, and the last I heard was divorced and drinking heavily. At the time I just accepted that's the way she was. But after looking at the studies that have been done, I can see she closely matches the statistics.

Of course, you won't let this happen to your children. You love them and want the best for them. Yes, you know the divorce will be hard, but you truly believe they'll adjust. You've been told that children are resilient. You honestly think you'll be able to help them cope with their short-lived pain. You've even read that when you get away from this intolerable situation and begin to heal, you'll be a better parent. Life in the short run will be hard, but you truly believe that in the long run divorce will be better for everyone.

On Monday evenings a group called Pieces to Peace meets at my church. It's designed to help children cope with their parents' divorce. They blame themselves and tend to think if they'd kept their room cleaner, been more obedient, or done better in school, their parents wouldn't have divorced. They are swept by over-whelming feelings of guilt. There is another feeling that can be even more destructive if not dealt with—anger. The custodial parent usually bears the brunt of it.

According to the American Academy of Pediatrics, divorce is like a death to a child and carries with it deep feelings of sadness and loss.[17] You may be thinking that their pain is short-lived and they will get over it, but the studies show that isn't true.

Judith Wallerstein followed a group of 131 children of divorce for twenty-five years. Eighteen months after the breakup, the divorce was still the central event of their lives; she didn't see a single child who was well adjusted. Five years later, she found a third of the children experienced moderate or severe depression, and at ten years a signif-icant number were drifting and underachieving. Even after twenty-five years, over half of the now-grown children had psychological problems they attributed to the divorce.[18]

Other studies have shown that children of divorce are more likely to experience emotional and behavioral problems, become pregnant as teenagers, abuse drugs, and get in trouble with the law. They are less successful as adults particularly in two domains: love and work. They have a harder time achieving intimacy or even holding a steady job.[19]

These children on average do poorly in reading, spelling, and math and are twice as likely to drop out of high school.[20] They also are less likely to apply for college.[21] They rate higher in depend-ency, anxiety, and aggressiveness, and lower in self-control. They rate low in peer popularity. They also score low in physical health and well-being. Sixty percent of rapists, 72 percent of adolescent murderers, and 70 percent of long-term prison inmates come from fatherless homes. They suffer much higher rates of both physical and sexual abuse, in the latter case most often carried out by the mother's boyfriend or their stepfather. Single mothers report being much more violent toward their children than do mothers in intact families.[22]

Among white families, daughters of single parents are 53 percent more likely to marry as teenagers, 111 percent more likely to have children as teenagers, 164 percent more likely to have a premarital birth, and 92 percent more likely to dissolve their own marriages.[23] One of the top ten reasons given in a recent Gallup poll for teenage suicides was the breakup of the family.

Better for the children? I think the statistics are clear. I've met only one adult child of divorce who told me it was for the best. However, she failed to mention that she has been in counseling a number of times for depression, was treated for ulcers as a child, and struggles today with the need to overachieve.

But these are statistics and your children are different? Perhaps you're right, but are any of these worth the risk?

Friends of ours tried to make their marriage work. They went for counseling and attended several different marriage retreats, but nothing seemed to work. Then one day after a terrible fight, he left. Their two daughters were devastated. They couldn't sleep and cried all the time. One of them became verbally abusive toward their mother, blaming her for the breakup. It affected their schoolwork, and the older one started staying out all night. I spent hours on the phone with the mother listening to the horror that her life had become and the nightmare her children were living through. One day we ran into her husband at a restaurant. He announced almost proudly the reason he'd left his wife: He'd done it for the children.

This man was so wrapped up in himself that he was totally oblivious to the havoc he'd wreaked. Take a good look at your children, and make sure this doesn't describe you.

Lie #3. It will be better for your husband.

Statistics show that divorce carries some economic good news for men. While most women see a drop in their standard of living, most men see an increase.[24] Their incomes, on the average, increase 10 to 15 percent after the divorce.[25] However, that's the end of the good news. Divorce is a life-changing event for the man too. He often will lose his home, his friends, and even his children. According to the National Survey of Children, of those whose parents had divorced, only one child in six saw his or her father as often as once a week in the past year. Half had not seen their father at all. As time goes on, contact becomes even less frequent. Ten years after a marriage breakup, more than two-thirds of children report not having seen their father for a year.[26]

One man I know moved to Texas in order to take a better job after his divorce. He hasn't seen his son in ten years. He wasn't there to teach him to drive or help him cope with failing a grade in junior high. He wasn't there for his first formal dance and didn't even make it home for his son's high-school graduation.

Only 20 percent of children in single-parent families named their father as a person they looked up to. Divorced fathers often become "treat" dads.[27] One young man recently asked an older Christian man to help him. He needed someone who could hold him accountable while he tried to get off drugs. Where was his father? He said he didn't have a dad, just a man who lived in California whom he saw once a year.

Emotionally the divorce may be harder on him than you. According to a report in the *American Journal of Psychiatry*, divorcing men are more than three times as likely to be clinically depressed than the average population. This depression, if it goes untreated, is "as dangerous as severe heart disease."[28]

We often think our husbands will get over a divorce quickly because they don't show their emotions. They seem wrapped up in their jobs, their hobbies, or their sports. We know they hate the fights, and we judge they feel as helpless as we do in figuring out what to do to fix a relationship that's gone sour. But I think we underestimate how much we mean to the man we pledged to love, honor, and obey. I know of two cases where husbands committed suicide after their wives left them. Another man I know went into a deep depression, was unable to work, and became homeless. My own brother who has a good job, a nice home, is tall and good looking, has trouble meeting women. He is lonely and wants his life to be different. And the man who told me he divorced his wife for the sake of the children? Just before the divorce was finalized, he begged his wife to take him back. He thought getting away was the answer, but once he left, the reality of how much his family meant to him hit him like a slap across the face. Sadly, his wife said no.

Recently I spoke to a group called Healing for Wounded Marriages. These are men and women whose spouses have left them. They meet every Monday for prayer and fellowship, believing together that God will restore their marriages. I noticed that all the men had sunken eyes. They had made mistakes and were desperate for another chance. One man said he'd been there for seven years.

When I was in your shoes, I wouldn't have wanted to know these facts. My mind was pretty well made up, and I didn't want to be dissuaded. This is hard stuff. If you are contemplating divorce, you're in a lot of pain. You want to do what is right, but you're hurting—unbearably at times. You find yourself crying over small things and hate the way you're behaving. What you want is for someone to hold you until it all goes away. You think there isn't another answer. But there is; I know because I found it. I don't want to leave you in the mess you're in. I want you to find the love you want, not through a divorce, but in your own marriage. You don't need to tear apart your life and the lives of the people you love most.

You might be saying right now that I don't know what your husband has done. I don't know the pain he's caused. You're right, I don't know. All I know is what I experienced and what other women have shared with me. In the next chapters, I'll share the key to finding real peace in your life whether you decide to stay or not.

❧

Action item: Pray the following prayer:

My friend, let go of yourself and you will find me.
If you wholly give yourself into my hands
And take nothing back
You shall have me.

Some persons surrender themselves to me,
But they hold something back.
They do not trust me fully,
And go on trying to provide for themselves.

Others, at the beginning,
offer all of themselves to me,
but when a difficult time comes they put their trust back in
themselves.

Such persons will never know perfect peace
And freedom of heart.

Give all for all
And hold back nothing.

Stand purely and strongly and steadfastly in me
And you shall have me.
You shall be so free in heart and in soul
That darkness shall never have power over you.

Seek out—study—pray for this freedom of spirit
That I speak of.

Seek always in your heart
To be free of everything that binds you,
That in love you may die to yourself
And to all worldly things
And blessedly live to me.

If you do this
All unimportant questions
Shall fail and fade and go away.
Crippling fear and misplaced love shall die in you.
You shall live in me and I in you.
> —THOMAS À KEMPIS, *THE IMITATION OF CHRIST*[29]

CHAPTER THREE

You Don't Know
How Bad Things Are

*Loneliness and the feeling of being unwanted
is the most terrible poverty.*
MOTHER TERESA[1]

*Y*ou're right, I don't know how bad things are. I don't know the
trouble your husband has caused, but I do know that you're hurting. It's a deep pain that causes you to rise up in anger, sometimes
over trivial things. It colors everything you do, everything you read,
everything you hear, and every word that comes out of your mouth.
You're tired of the same old arguments. Your evenings are strained;
you probably don't even want him to come home at night. His
touch seems insincere, and you sleep with your backs to each other.
When you reach out to your husband for love and understanding,
you're disappointed. He's just not there for you.

I also know of your loneliness. You look across the table at your
husband and long to tell him of your pain, but you can't. He just
doesn't understand.

But this isn't how it always was. Remember when you first met?

You couldn't get enough of each other. He was thoughtful, interesting, and fun. He made you feel like the most important person in the world. You spent every day trying to figure out how to spend time together. You went on picnics, studied together in the library, sat in the sand on the beach telling each other your innermost secrets. You spent long hours staring into each other's eyes, talking, and touching.

Where did all those wonderful feelings go?

Leslie told me that she doesn't think she ever loved her husband. Monica said she had doubts from the start, and now she wishes she had paid more attention to them. Deborah said she only married her husband because he was nice to her daughter. I decided that what I had felt was only infatuation, not true love. If we'd dated longer, we would never have married.

These stories have one thing in common: It's hard to remember what we were feeling in the past because our memories are colored by how we're feeling right now. In my case I was trying to justify my decision. In retrospect, I've come to believe that my feelings of love were real; they were just lost.

They disappeared not in the heat of a single battle, but at the bottom of a wall I could not climb. The wall was made mostly of minor things. Busy schedules, financial woes, waiting for phone calls that never came, repeated thoughtless acts, unresolved fights, differences that chafed us raw, chores that went undone, broken promises, and hurtful remarks. I could fill a book with the wrongs committed by my husband, and I'm sure you could too.

I remember clearly the day I laid the first brick. We had been married about nine months. We went to a movie with friends. I waited in anticipation for Larry to reach over and take my hand to prove to me that the magic was still there. But he didn't. And as the movie continued, I grew hurt and then angry. By the time the final credits rolled across the screen, I was furious. He shrugged it off, surprised that I was so upset over such a little thing. To him it was nothing; to me it was the first sign that our love wasn't perfect.

As time wore on, I laid more bricks. A present given at Christmas that was less than I expected. Although I'd pretend to love it, I secretly felt hurt. When we first married, he called me every day from work. Slowly those phone calls grew farther and farther apart, until they stopped altogether. When I brought it up, he'd start calling again, but it wasn't the same. He was only doing it because I'd complained and he wanted to keep me happy, not because he *wanted* to call me. Once I griped about his lack of romance and suggested he give me a card. For the next six months he showered me with cards that dripped with sentimental words that meant less and less with each one. He tried to make me happy, but his motive ruined everything he tried.

In the evening when we watched TV, he'd fall asleep. When we went out for dinner, he couldn't think of anything to say. His days off were measured by how much he got done. Chores took priority, his work took priority, the children took priority. I was at the bottom of his list. I got the crumbs, and I was starving.

I begged God to change him, or to change me, but the pain grew with each passing year. I remember the day I sat on the couch and told myself I'd have to stop caring so much. I'd have to quit wanting him, and I steeled myself against any sexual desire.

The decision to leave your husband is not made in a moment; it's arrived at over time. Evidence has to be gathered until there's enough so that people will say it's the right thing to do; it was the only thing you could do; what you've done is totally justified. The tearing apart of what God has put together is a heartless act, and in order to do it you have to be determined. You have to stop caring, because to care would mean you have to stay. In order to leave, you have to build a wall around your heart.

Oh yes, like you, we tried. We read books; we talked to our pastor who referred us to another pastor who then referred us to a professional counselor. Nothing worked because I had hardened my heart. It was like our front yard. Every spring the lawn was beautiful, but starting in June it would begin to die and by July it was brown. To make it worse, the neighbors' lawns were a beautiful green. We watered it regularly, but instead of soaking in, the water ran down the sidewalk and out into the street. We eventually pulled the lawn up and discovered that under the thin layer of grass was a hard, impenetrable layer of clay. Nothing could get past it, not even the life-saving water. That is a good picture of what my heart had become.

In Matthew, Jesus says, "Moses provided for divorce as a concession to your hardheartedness, but it is not part of God's original plan."[2] My mind was made up, and I wasn't going to let anything deter me.

If you identify with what I'm saying, then I want to offer you hope. God softened my heart, and he can soften yours. Jesus says, "The thief comes only to steal and kill and destroy; I have come that [you] may have life, and have it to the full."[3] Divorce seems like the answer right now, the only answer, but that would be choosing the easy way out. Christian psychiatrist Paul D. Meier says that it's "the greatest cop-out and by far the most immature choice."[4]

It takes great courage and maturity to stay and work. I'm here to tell you that you can have the marriage you've always dreamed about, the love you've always desired. You don't have to live like this any longer, and you don't have to pull your family apart. Here's how.

1. Recognize your part.

The first step is to recognize your part in the unhappiness of your marriage. It feels good to blame your husband for your problems. None of us like to admit that we're guilty. Even murderers stand before judges and claim they are innocent, not because they are but because they're trying to justify their sins. And that's what I did. I was miserable and wanted to blame Larry. It was his fault. If only he'd do this, if only he'd do that. I had a long laundry list of changes I wanted him to make. I was completely blinded by my own sin.

My hard heart had done more to damage our relationship than

anything he'd done. The Bible talks about getting the log out of your eye so you can see to take the speck out of your brother's eye.[5] My hard heart rejected everything Larry tried. Instead of seeing Larry's cards as an attempt to make me happy, I saw them as a weak attempt to keep the peace, a quick fix. I began to think of myself as superior, wiser, and more discerning. I'd ridicule his ideas and ignore his reasoning. Nothing he did was good enough. Instead of his strengths, I majored on his weaknesses. When he'd try to do what I'd ask, I'd be sarcastic because it wasn't enough.

I was destroying the man I loved and the father of my children.

Recently I saw this behavior reflected in the life of a man I know. Two years ago he decided his wife no longer met his needs, and so he slowly started to pull away from her until he reached the point where he could leave. He moved in with another woman. His wife and children are devastated, but he seemingly doesn't care. I know he does care, but he had to insulate himself in order to leave. The children want to contact him, but he doesn't even answer their phone calls. He's afraid they might break the hard shell he's so painstakingly built around his heart.

I know because that's how I was. I had pretty much given up hope when, as a last resort, I agreed to attend a Marriage Encounter weekend. I went believing that when it was over, I would walk away from my marriage. However, God had other plans. On that weekend, he kindly and lovingly confronted me with my sin. As I listened to other couples share their stories, my heart melted. All of my carefully built reasoning and excuses were crushed under his loving hand. I realized divorce wasn't what I wanted. What I wanted was to love and be loved by my husband. However, as long as I remained hardhearted, that would never happen.

2. Pray for forgiveness.
If you can see that you have done the same thing, then let me walk you through the steps from anger to peace. Remember that lawn?

The only thing we could do was to throw it away and start over. We brought in good topsoil and mixed it into the clay and sand. Today we have a beautiful lawn year-round. It began with the tearing up. That's what you need to do to your heart. You need to tear out the old hard layer so God can work in you to create a beautiful life— one that's full of joy and peace and love.

Make a quiet place right now and ask for God's forgiveness. Confess what you've done. Be as specific as you can. When you ask, don't do it lightly. Do it with an attitude that you want to change.

Some of you don't believe you can do it. You're afraid to let go. Your shell has become your protection. Without it you fear you'll be vulnerable again. I can't take this step for you; you have to decide to do it yourself. You have to dig deep into yourself and dredge up the last vestiges of your faith. You must believe that God won't let you crash at the bottom, but will scoop you up into his loving arms.

Picture this. In Psalms it says we are surrounded by angels.[6] Think of them surrounding you right now. They're cheering for you. "Go, go, go," they're shouting, for they know that when you do, it will be a victory for God and the defeat of Satan.

I remember the day I let go. I was alone in my living room, kneeling by the fireplace. I was truly convicted of how damaging my behavior had been. I sobbed as I, for the first time, realized that I played a big part in my own unhappiness and was destroying the man I loved. I saw my sin. This is called conviction. True forgiveness begins at this moment. Then and only then do we know what to ask forgiveness for and we can determine in our hearts to change our behavior.

In 1 John it says, "If we say that we have no sin, we deceive ourselves, and the truth is not in us. If we confess our sins, He is faithful and just to forgive us our sins and to cleanse us from all unrighteousness."[7] When I asked for God's forgiveness, he took away my shame and restored my relationship with him. I got up off my knees a new creation.

Change began in me that moment. Not in my power, but in God's. Each believer has the Holy Spirit living in her. I like to remember that I have Jesus Christ inside me, helping me, urging me to grow and change and reminding me when I slip back into old behaviors. Every time I've tried to change myself, I've failed. Every time I let God change me, I've succeeded. And you can too. "Simply embrace what the Spirit is doing in [you]."[8]

If I were with you right now, I'd take your hand and pray with you. I would cry with you and praise God for this new beginning. I would also tell you not to expect too much from yourself just yet. The changes will happen slowly; just as our yard took lots of hard work and time, the changes in your heart will require the same. The good news is God is waiting to help you. He wants to give you a clean heart. He wants to wash you with his love. He walked me through these steps, slowly, so I would learn as I went. I won't tell you this will be easy. It won't be. It will call for you to deny yourself; it will call for courage; it will call for unbelievable faith. Let me encourage you, every time I called on God to help me, he was there. "Those who trust God's action in them find that God's Spirit is in them—living and breathing God!"[9]

You may have to return to your knees more than once. That's okay too. Forgiveness is often a process, like peeling the layers off an onion.

You will know when you're ready to take this step. A premature confession probably won't lead to the peace that I discovered. Perhaps the best you can do now is say that you'll be open to reading the rest of this book. Pray about it, asking for God's guidance and for his timing.

Some of you are probably asking why you have to be the one to make the changes. What about your husband? Someone has to take that first step. And when you do, you will discover that your husband will have to change in response. It's as if you've both been dancing the same way for years. When one of you begins to do a tango instead of a waltz, the other has to change, too, or get his feet stepped on. I thought Larry would never become the husband that I wanted, but he did. It began with my willingness to change.

ॐ

Action item: Read Matthew 11:28–30 and pray that God will prepare your heart so you can forgive.

CHAPTER FOUR

You Don't Know My Husband

*When men and women are able to respect and accept their
differences then love has a chance to blossom.*
JOHN GRAY, PH.D.[1]

Recently a young woman I work with told me she and her husband would never have any problems because they were so much alike. I had to laugh because I remember saying almost exactly those words. I truly believed we were as alike as two peas in a pod. And we were alike in a lot of ways, but I didn't appreciate our differences until it was almost too late.

In the seventies there was a popular song that cried, "I am woman hear me roar." We reached for our potential, not caring who we trampled along the way. Power was within our grasp; all we had to do was grab it. It was heady stuff and, like a lot of women, I bought into it. Along with this newfound power was the message that men and women were alike and that there were no differences between the sexes. If you look at old pictures from those days you'll notice we even dressed alike. (Larry and I had matching green and gold tie-dyed T-shirts and bell-bottom pants. We were real groovy.)

In the nineties, the experts have discovered something "new." Men and women are not alike. John Gray's book *Men Are from Mars, Women Are from Venus* was on the bestsellers list for months. In it he points out that the two sexes are like two different species, one from Mars and the other from Venus. We look alike and use the same language, but in all other respects we are aliens to each other.[2] In general, when a woman wants to know what she thinks, she talks out loud. A man, on the other hand, withdraws into his cave to mull over all of the possibilities before he speaks. Women tend to be more feeling-oriented, men action-oriented. When a woman comes to her husband to share a problem, his first reaction is to fix it, which frustrates her to no end because all she wanted was to talk about her problem and come to her own solution. Problems arise because we don't recognize our differences. Of course, I don't think you can categorize people into such neat little boxes, but there is a lot of truth in his book. We *are* different.

Patrick Morley, in his book *What Husbands Wish Their Wives Knew about Men*, lists seven characteristics that our husbands have in common.

1. You are probably your husband's only friend.
2. He doesn't think anyone cares about him.
3. His deepest need is for significance.
4. He shows his feelings with actions rather than words.
5. He's under a lot of pressure.
6. What he needs most is companionship and support.
7. He's a product of his home.[3]

Let's take a brief look at each of these points. As we do, think about your own husband and what he's like. Try to get inside his skin and understand him. I don't think you can know your husband until you can do this.

1. You are probably your husband's only friend.
This might surprise you, but even if your husband is distant and cold, you probably are the closest friend he has. Few men have what we would consider true friends. They may have drinking buddies or fishing buddies or golfing buddies, but these are not deep, intimate relationships. He has no one to share his dreams, his fears, or his joys. All he has is you.

Once my husband told me he was jealous of the friends I have and that he'd give anything to have another man he could open up to. When I ask myself what kind of friend I am to my husband, the answer is very convicting.

2. He doesn't think anyone cares about him.
We're all so busy running here and running there that there's little time for more than surface communication. You probably both work and may not even have the same schedules. I have friends who work in the evening and whose husbands work during the day so they can share childcare responsibilities. I have a coworker who is constantly trying to change her schedule to match her husband's, only to have it changed again. For years my husband has worked at least two nights every week. (Now he's a pastor and at times he's gone even more nights than before.)

If you have children they are probably involved in baseball, ballet, tennis, music lessons, or a myriad of other activities that are available to them. In the evening there are PTA meetings, Boy Scout meetings, Camp Fire Girl meetings, and church services. There's the TV, the Internet, computer games, the newspaper, or a good book to bury ourselves in that takes us away from each other. We're all running this way and that. We women crave a moment when someone gives us a hug and asks how we are and means it. Does someone do that for your husband? Do you?

3. His deepest need is for significance.

Your husband has a deep desire to make a difference in the world. He wants to know that his life meant something. For years my husband was unhappy working in retail because he could find nothing meaningful about selling clothing. He hated going to work and was exhausted when he got home, not from fatigue as much as from a deep weariness born out of doing something he didn't like. Living with an unhappy husband is a real challenge. He did his best to keep his chin up, but when things would get tough at work, he would bring it home. He often withdrew into television or slept away his day off, too bone-weary from a job where he didn't feel appreciated or valued. How do you encourage your husband in his work?

4. He shows his feelings with actions rather than words.

We long to have our husbands tell us we are loved and cherished. We crave deep, intimate conversations and feel disappointed when this doesn't happen. Yes, you might have experienced these moments during your dating years, but this is not a natural state for a man. He tends to drift back to his natural way of showing his feelings— through actions. When he fixes the leaking faucet, he's saying, I love and care for you. When he goes to work, he's saying, I think you are special. When he brings home a paycheck, he may see it as the highest form of love. Even though Larry doesn't drink coffee, he fixes mine every morning. It's his way of saying to me that I am cherished. I hope I never take it for granted.

The reverse is also true. All of my words mean nothing to him if they're not followed up with actions. Cleaning house, fixing his favorite meal, or wearing something he considers sexy says more to him than all the "I love you's" in the world.

5. *He's under a lot of pressure.*

There's not enough time to do all the things your husband would like to do, all the things you want him to do, and all the things he thinks he should do. He feels guilty for not spending more time with the kids and you, but he also feels guilty for not spending enough time at work or at the church. Right now our two sons are in college, but Larry is still torn four ways. The first area pertains to his responsibilities at the church. He just started a new job as a counseling pastor. He's putting in incredible hours and feeling the pressure of doing everything well. He's also an elder, which entails more meetings during the week, special requests for prayers, hospital visits, and phone calls. Another commitment is his mother. She has recently moved to an assisted-living center and needs lots of attention. His third area of concern is his home. He has a yard to maintain and a house that needs repairs. Finally, there's me. We're all vying for his attention, and there's just not enough of him to go around.

Your husband also worries about money. He's probably making enough now to pay the bills, but ahead looms college tuition, retirement, or a car that needs to be replaced. Maybe you live in an apartment or condo and you dream about owning your own home. He might not admit he's worrying about these things, but his stomach may clench with every TV commercial dealing with the cost of tuition and the need to save. If there's debt, it probably keeps him awake at night or may be the reason he's guzzling Mylanta after every meal.

He probably worries about his job. The economy is good as I write this, but companies are continually downsizing. I just read where personal bankruptcy is at an all-time high. New technology is making some jobs obsolete. Years afterward my husband told me about a time when his company was laying people off. Every day when he went to work, he was scared that he'd be fired. He said he didn't want me to worry, so he didn't share his fear.

Morley says, "A man's most conscious fear . . . is that he will not be able to provide for his family."[4] Do you ever thank your husband for going to work every day?

Did you know that "men (today) are tired—mentally, emotionally, physically, and spiritually tired. Weary of life."[5] What are you doing to ease this burden for your husband?

6. What he needs most is companionship and support.

Do you encourage your husband or discourage him? Are you fun to be around? Do you help your husband relax? Do you support his decisions or argue with them? When he fails, do you point it out? Do you tell him all the things he does wrong? Men are not as emotionally strong as they pretend. They need us much more than they'll ever say. Do you greet him with a smile when he comes home from work? Such a simple thing, but it can set the tone for the whole evening. Do you enjoy the things he does? Have you even tried?

I like watching football, but it took me years to learn the game. The more I know about it, the more I enjoy it. In fact, now I'm a bigger fan than Larry is. Be interested in what he's interested in. You can learn to golf or bowl. Or seek something mutual that you can do together. Dr. James Dobson says that he and his family took up skiing. We like shopping for antiques and browsing through shops in the small tourist towns around Seattle. This kind of outing leads to more conversation than we have when we're at home distracted by all the pressing chores.

7. He's a product of his home.

One of the biggest needs your husband has is to make his daddy proud. Even if his father is dead, was abusive, alcoholic, or was never around, that drive is the motive behind most of what he does. One of the most important steps in healing my marriage was to understand this.

My husband's childhood was difficult. He was born with a physical handicap that caused his left foot to turn in and down. He was unable to place his foot flat on the ground. When he was seven years old he was put on a train and sent alone to Portland, Oregon, to undergo major reconstructive surgery. How scared and lonely he must've been as he lay there in a hospital bed all by himself facing the unknowns of surgery. Who was there to comfort him when he woke up in pain? Who was there to tell him he was loved and cared for? No one. They sent him home with a brace on his leg, which mortified him. He wanted so badly to be like the rest of the kids, but he was different.

His father jokingly told him he was stupid and no good and that he'd never amount to anything. I try to imagine this overly sensitive child growing up into a man with that voice playing in the back of his mind. I'm sure it was a small voice and hardly audible as he became the first in his family to attend college, graduated, and got his first job. The negative voice almost disappeared during our courtship and the first years of our marriage as he was promoted often.

When he made mistakes or didn't live up to my expectations, I'm sure the voice was there confirming what his father had told him many years earlier. When I think about his childhood, I understand why he couldn't reach out and comfort me when I hurt. Who had comforted him? Who had shown him how? The love I craved from him had never been modeled. How could he be what I wanted him to be when he had no idea what that looked like?

When I imagine his heart, I see it bruised and beaten and full of longing to be told he's loved and that someone is proud of him. But what did I do? I told him that I didn't love him anymore. I told him with my words and actions that he wasn't good enough for me. I beat him down just as surely as his father had.

I made lots of assumptions about why Larry was doing the things he was doing. Most of them were negative—he didn't care about the children or me, he was selfish and stubborn and had no backbone. Sometimes he was downright mean. I couldn't see the real Larry Bodmer because I was too close. It was like putting my nose up against a van Gogh. From that distance you can see the brush strokes, the unevenness of the lines, and colors that don't make any sense. But when you step back, you can see the whole and feel the emotional impact. Maybe it's time to step back and look at the heart of the man you married.

Take out a piece of paper and write what you know about your husband's life. Start with his childhood and try to imagine what it was like. If you don't know the details, then begin to ask. Don't push, be gentle. Good times to talk about these things are when you're driving in the car or out to dinner or taking a walk. Intimate conversation can be very hard for some men, so don't be surprised if he seems uncomfortable. Listen carefully to what he's saying, and to what he's *not* saying. Look at his negatives and ask yourself why. Why does he behave this way? If he brags too much about his accomplishments, perhaps it's because he doesn't feel significant.

There's an old Indian legend that says you don't know a man until you walk two moons in his moccasins. Become a student of your husband.

❧

Action item: You and your spouse draw a picture of the home you grew up in. (If you moved a lot, use the one you liked the most.) Put a star by the place where you most enjoyed spending time. Tell each other why. Now draw a picture of your present home and do the same thing.

CHAPTER FIVE

I Can't Forgive or Forget

Create in me a clean heart, O God, and . . .
Restore to me the joy of Your salvation.
PSALM 51:10, 12, NKJV

*W*hen I was in college I worked part-time as a diet aide in the Continuing Care Unit of a local hospital. Most of the patients were difficult to work with and would blow up over little things. Their coffee wasn't hot enough, the salt had been left off their tray, or they got chicken on their dinner tray instead of spaghetti. One man had a stroke and the only speech he retained was swearwords. I began to understand why visitors stayed away. Many of these patients had good cause to be angry; they were ill, away from their loved ones, and unable to do any of the things that made them feel useful.

There was one exception—Mr. Jensen. He had every right to be as angry as the others. He'd had a stroke and was confined to a wheelchair. He mumbled when he talked and drooled out of one side of his mouth. I learned that he had been a wealthy businessman and owned several buildings in one of the major business areas of

Seattle. His wealth and power had been reduced to a hospital room he shared with another man and a bedside table where he kept his few belongings. And yet he never complained. Instead his face shone with a half smile that warmed the entire wing of the hospital. When he saw me, he would reach out his crippled hand, take mine, and mumble sweet words of encouragement.

I was young, far from God, and yet I saw the difference and vowed that when I got old, I'd be like Mr. Jensen. The years passed. I finished my education; we bought a house, started going to church regularly, and had two babies in two years. It became more difficult to be that person. I had two in diapers, a house that always seemed dirty, a husband who was immersed in his own business, and bills that we couldn't pay.

I kept up a good outward appearance. To people at church and my neighbors, I said the right things. But on the inside I was having a hard time maintaining control. When I least expected, this ugly side of me would burst forth. I snapped at store clerks. I blew up at my children. Comments made off the cuff buried themselves in my mind where they festered and grew into major wounds. One small misstep by Larry and I would let him have it. We had ugly fights. This monster lived in me and when it emerged, I said horrible, hateful things. It seemed that the harder I tried to keep that side of me hidden, the worse I grew. I avoided people, afraid they would discover the real me.

What happened to my good intentions? Why couldn't I be like Mr. Jensen? The reasons are complex, but the most important one is *I never learned to forgive.*

In a previous chapter I told you that God gave Larry and me a new beginning in our relationship. For a while it was like a honeymoon. Our passion for each other returned. We laughed and shared things openly and honestly for the first time in years.

But just like someone who loses twenty pounds and gains it back, I slipped back into my old habits. I had a lot to learn and God had a lot to teach me. His lessons often came at unexpected times—while reading a book, listening to a radio program, or talking with a friend. One of the most memorable lessons came as I sat in church, Larry beside me. Our pastor began his sermon with the following story:

A couple came to him for counseling. As far as he knew they were happily married. That's why he was surprised when the wife said she wanted to leave her husband. When asked why, she said, "I can't take the black book anymore." The pastor was momentarily confused, thinking she was referring to the Bible. "No, show him," she said. The husband drew a small black book out of his pocket. In it he'd made a list of everything she'd done wrong since the day they married.

The audience gasped, but I don't think anyone was as upset as I was. I searched the sea of faces wondering if it was someone I knew. If it was, I'd give him a piece of my mind. This man was despicable; no wonder his wife wanted to leave him. The rest of the sermon was lost on me as my mind raced with indignity. Then from somewhere a still, small voice said, "But aren't you guilty of the same thing? You might not write them in a book, but don't you keep track in your head of every wrong your husband ever committed?"

I was guilty, as guilty as that man I had wanted to throttle just a few minutes earlier. Inside of me was an ugly, hateful thing—an unforgiving heart.

WHY IS IT SO HARD TO FORGIVE?

I don't know about you, but I can identify at least four reasons why I don't forgive. First, I'm a nice person. Let me tell you about nice people. We aren't honest. We tell lies to keep the peace. We ignore our true feelings and replace them with what we should be feeling. We don't deal with little irritations or say aloud what we're thinking, afraid it might hurt someone's feelings. We want people to like us. Fitting in is the most important thing. Confrontation is to be avoided at all cost. We think it's for the best.

But in reality, we never deal with issues head-on. We never let them come out into the open where they can be discussed and resolved and forgiven.

I was one of seven children. We didn't have much growing up, but my parents tried their best to buy us treats. I remember one time when Dad stopped at a drive-in restaurant for ice cream. We shouted the flavors we wanted: chocolate, vanilla, and strawberry. (This was before the days of thirty-two flavors.) He returned with seven cones, all of them vanilla. It wasn't what I wanted, but I didn't say anything. I was just glad to get ice cream.

My little sister sat next to me, her arms crossed and her mouth set. When Dad offered a cone to her, she shook her head. We all froze. Dad was clearly angry.

"I wanted strawberry," she said.

"You'll have vanilla," he said.

"Then I don't want any," she said.

I was shocked at her courage. How could she stand up to our father who in my mind was God? You didn't do anything that went against him, including refusing to take ice cream. Afraid for her, I nudged her to take it. She shook her head.

"I'll take it," said one of my brothers from the backseat, and before we knew it the cone was claimed and the crisis over. That incident shows how early the pattern was set in me. You don't speak up. You accept what's given to you. You bury your desires for the sake of peace. You don't do anything that will make Dad mad.

I used to think my sister was crazy, but now I can see that her way was a lot healthier. My way led me into a lifelong behavior that was destructive, but I didn't recognize it. I thought I was doing what was best—to keep the peace. Let me show you what this looks like in an everyday situation.

Dinner is ready; Matthew and David are fighting over the rules of Monopoly in the other room. Larry is late getting home from work again after he promised to be on time. I look out the window. Where is he? He should be here. I'm hungry; I'm tired; I'm angry. But Christian women don't get angry; they are patient and kind and loving. When my husband walks in, I stuff all my negative feelings and greet him with a kiss and a somewhat stiff smile. We sit down to eat. He tells me about his day, all the troubles he had, how bad the traffic was. I listen and wait for him to ask about me, about my day. I don't say it aloud because that's selfish. He's in a hurry; he has a meeting at church. He goes off to change. I'm left with the dishes and two boys who are complaining about what I fixed for dinner. I'm hurt; I'm alone. I have another piece of cake.

The next morning I awaken to the sound of the garbage truck going up our street. Larry has forgotten to put the cans out again. Later, I get into the car to go to work. The gas tank is empty, which means I'll be late. Larry drove it last, why couldn't he have warned me? That evening Larry, sensing the tension in me that I'm not even aware of, asks if anything is wrong. I say no, and I want to mean it. I want it to be true, I want to be that super-Christian woman who can take it all. The truth is I'm angry and I'm hurt, but I don't know how to handle my negative emotions without blowing everyone's evening. And so I swallow the truth and I become more the person I don't want to be.

Second, I couldn't forgive because forgiving meant letting go of the wrongs that had been done to me. I'd been hurt time and time again. Someone needed to pay for the way I'd been treated, for the disappointments that I'd suffered, for the deep loneliness that made every day almost unbearable.

In Matthew there is a story that speaks to this attitude:

> Then Peter came to Jesus and asked, "Lord, how many times shall I forgive my brother when he sins against me? Up to seven times?"

Jesus answered, "I tell you, not seven times, but seventy-seven times.

"Therefore, the kingdom of heaven is like a king who wanted to settle accounts with his servants. As he began the settlement, a man who owed him ten thousand talents was brought to him. Since he was not able to pay, the master ordered that he and his wife and his children and all that he had be sold to repay the debt.

"The servant fell on his knees before him. 'Be patient with me,' he begged, 'and I will pay back everything.' The servant's master took pity on him, canceled the debt and let him go.

"But when that servant went out, he found one of his fellow servants who owed him a hundred denarii. He grabbed him and began to choke him. 'Pay back what you owe me!' he demanded.

"His fellow servant fell to his knees and begged him, 'Be patient with me, and I will pay you back.'

"But he refused. Instead, he went off and had the man thrown into prison until he could pay the debt. When the other servants saw what had happened, they were greatly distressed and went and told their master everything that had happened.

"Then the master called the servant in. 'You wicked servant,' he said, 'I canceled all that debt of yours because you begged me to. Shouldn't you have had mercy on your fellow servant just as I had on you?' In anger his master turned him over to the jailers to be tortured, until he should pay back all he owed.

"This is how my heavenly Father will treat each of you unless you forgive your brother from your heart."

MATTHEW 18:21–35

I was the first servant. I accepted God's forgiveness for my sins, which were many, and in turn I would not forgive my husband for his sins, which were small in comparison. I held my husband to a different standard from the one I held myself to.

One of the best parts about falling in love is discovering someone who loves you completely and accepts both your good and bad qualities. That's what I wanted most from my husband, but that's not what I was willing to give him. I did not, in fact would not, give him the same grace I was asking from God and from him.

Your husband needs your forgiveness even if he doesn't ask for it, and even though he doesn't deserve it. He needs you to forgive him for:

- Making mistakes
- Being tired
- Not responding to your sexual advances
- Not being able to give you the one thing we need most, intimacy
- Not building you up
- Not being happy
- Being prideful and not being able to admit his faults and mistakes
- Believing he's self-sufficient
- Being difficult
- Not being the man he promised to be during courtship
- How he handles his anger—whether he avoids you, holds grudges, or explodes
- Being human

Third, I didn't forgive because Larry never asked to be forgiven. Both Larry and I are passive peacemakers, and we never learned to fight the right way. We buried our anger until one of us exploded, usually me, and then we both dumped on each other. Nothing was ever resolved. We attacked each other, not the issue. In fact the issue got lost in the accusations. Who was right became the most important thing. Often our fights ended, not with reconciliation, but because it was 2:00 A.M. and we had to get some sleep.

Fourth, I couldn't forgive because then I would be forced to look at my own part in the breakup of our marriage. I wanted to be the victim. Victims aren't responsible. Other people are responsible. Other people have to change. This attitude can relieve a lot of guilt, but it won't make you happy or solve even one little problem in your life.

WHAT ARE THE SYMPTOMS OF AN UNFORGIVING HEART?

Do these reasons sound familiar? Have you fallen into the same bad habits? Then maybe you, too, have an unforgiving heart. Listed below are a few of the symptoms:

1. Blowing up over seemingly small things
2. Sarcastic remarks that are meant to hurt
3. Talking about your husband to others
4. Criticizing
5. Correcting
6. Unexplained headaches, stomach problems, fatigue
7. A bout of tears for no apparent reason

I didn't want to be this way. I just couldn't seem to stop. In Matthew it says, ". . . out of the overflow of the *heart* the mouth speaks."[1] What's filling your heart? Mine was full of disappointment, resentment, bitterness, anger, pride, and sorrow. No matter how hard I tried to be a loving person on the outside, I was doomed to failure until I allowed God to cleanse what was in my heart. My unforgiving attitude was hurting me more than it was hurting Larry. It was turning me into the very person I'd vowed not to be so many years before.

An unforgiving heart keeps you from living life fully. It robs you of joy. It keeps you from seeing the real person you married because you're blinded by his past mistakes. It erodes what love you have left, and it keeps you from experiencing the fullness of your relationship. It also blocks your prayers and makes you feel that God is distant and uncaring.[2]

Even if you leave your husband, you will take your heart with you. The excitement of finding someone new and falling in love again might mask your unforgiving heart for a while, but eventually it will reappear.

It will affect all of your friendships. I worked with someone who was bitter. When I said, "Nice day," she'd say, "Looks like rain." When I said, "Look how long the days are," she'd say, "Won't be long and it'll be winter." No matter what I said that was positive, she'd come back with a negative. No one likes to be around a woman who does nothing but complain or always sees the negative side of things.

A bitter, negative attitude will drive your children away. So many angry, bitter people living in nursing homes today never have any visitors. Is this how you want to end your life?

WHAT DOES FORGIVENESS MEAN?

I have some good news. You can change; you can be different. But before we look at how, let's first look at what forgiveness means. Forgiveness is one of those things you have to experience. The best description I can come up with is a physical one. Clench your fist tightly. Now open it slowly until your hand is completely open. Feel the difference? That's a physical representation of what it means to forgive. A clenched fist is a symbol of anger and power, an open palm one of peace and friendship.

When I forgive I feel it in my shoulders and chest. It's the sensation of a big weight being lifted from them. This comes from releasing the anger and hurt that I have allowed to bind my heart and my mind.

Sometimes it's easy to forgive, but other times I find it more difficult. It's not always related to the size of the offense. Sometimes the little things are the hardest to forgive because they seem so thoughtless. Marcia once told me about her husband leaving his dirty socks on the floor. Now that seems like a small thing, hardly worth mentioning. I asked why she didn't just forget it and pick up the socks, and the suggestion infuriated her. It became obvious the socks on the floor meant something much bigger. They represented how he felt about her. If he loved her he would pick up his socks. She had begged, pleaded, and done everything she knew to try to get him to pick them up. And he still refused. Does this sound familiar? Maybe for you it's the toilet seat, the garbage, the newspaper, or the way he checks all the doors after you've already locked them.

For me it's my work schedule. I work part-time at a local library. Larry can never remember what days or hours I work, even though they are the same each week. This probably doesn't sound like such a big deal to you, but it hurts me that he can't remember. It has become more than forgetting; it has become a sign of his not caring for me. I've placed a different value on it. If he cared, he'd remember.

Forgiving means to cancel a debt. Pretend you own Visa or MasterCard and your husband owes you $25,000. Forgiving is stamping "Paid in Full" across the bill, even though he hasn't paid you a dime. It's a gift, and if done right there should be no strings attached. You can't go back and say, "Oops, I didn't mean to cancel that debt. You still owe it to me." You also can't wave it over his head and say, "I forgave you your debt, now you owe me gratitude big time." That's not a gift. That's a prison.

For this reason forgiveness should not be done lightly or too soon. Don't say, "I'm sorry" in the heat of the argument. Larry or I used to say this over and over, but we both knew we didn't mean it. We were just saying those words to end the fight.

On the other hand, don't wait until the hurt goes away completely before you forgive. That would be like canceling a debt that isn't owed at all. The hurt probably will never go away until you are willing to forgive. It's like a sore that's festering and full of infection, opened again and again. Forgiving is the healing balm. And like a healing it may take time.

Forgiveness means giving up the right to ever bring up the offense again or use it against your husband in any way. You can't present the bill again, once it has been canceled. Forgiving is a conscious action. You do it. It's deliberate and it has consequences. You can't bring it up ever again. Therefore, don't do it lightly.

Real forgiveness means you stop burying or writing offenses on a list. When I was in grade school, I would stay after and help the teacher clean the chalkboards. There were two kinds of erasers. The small, black felt ones would wipe some of the chalk away, but you could still read the words underneath. But there was another kind of eraser. It was foam rubber. It was my favorite because it wiped the boards completely clean. When I was done, they looked brand-new. Forgiving means using the foam-rubber eraser.

At first completely letting go of an offense was hard. I'd grown used to cherishing hurts in my heart and using them later as ammunition. Believe it or not, there's a lot of power derived from being the victim. It frees you from any responsibility and justifies anything you might want to do in retaliation.

I was told once by a recovering alcoholic that while he was drinking he would look for things to get angry about so he could drink without feeling guilty. These included things like dinner not being ready on time, the lawn not being mowed, or the TV being too loud. He told his wife and children that it was their fault. If they would just do everything right, then he wouldn't have to drown himself in a bottle. He was looking for something to get angry about. In effect I was doing the same thing. Being the victim freed me from any guilt I might have over my anger or the way I treated my husband. It was his fault, not mine.

For some of us letting go and never bringing up the offense

again is difficult. I was told recently about a woman whose husband had a sexual encounter with another woman. The wife was furious. She told everyone that her husband was an adulterer. She's even called him that in front of their children. Her husband is repentant, but she won't forgive. Her reaction has now become the greater problem. She's actually done more damage than the affair did.

Not ever bringing up the offense again can be a tough commitment and should be taken seriously. Before I forgive, I weigh the offense against this rule. There are times when I'm angry and I want to yell, "No, you don't deserve my forgiveness." There are times I have to say, "I'm sorry. I'm not ready yet." But I've learned that forgiving isn't just for my husband, it's for me too.[3]

Forgiving may mean telling the person he is forgiven in order to alleviate his guilt. Last summer my son borrowed $300 from me. At the time I wanted to just give it to him, but I didn't. Later I decided to forgive the debt because I could afford to, and he's putting himself through college working two jobs. I could've just let it go, but I came to realize that he probably was feeling guilty about not repaying the money, so I told him. I freed him from the guilt that he was feeling. The same is true when we forgive our spouses. We need to tell them we've forgiven them, especially if they're feeling guilty.

Don't use your forgiveness as a weapon. Yesterday Larry asked again, "Now what hours do you work today?" That old feeling of resentment raised its ugly head and I felt angry. From the look on his face it was clear that he was feeling guilty for not remembering. I could've said, "I forgive you for being thoughtless once again." Would that have been loving? No, it would've been cruel, even if I hadn't said the words aloud, but let them come through in my tone of voice. Instead I forgave him in my heart and then smiled and made a joke, easing the moment between us.

I hate this last aspect of forgiveness because it's the hardest part. Forgiveness means doing it over and over and over, no matter how often the offense is repeated. We're all familiar with the scripture in

Matthew that says, "Then Peter came to Him and said, 'Lord, how often shall my brother sin against me, and I forgive him? Up to seven times?' Jesus said to him, 'I do not say to you, up to seven times, but up to seventy times seven.'"⁴ Was Jesus saying we should forgive our husbands 490 times? No, the Greek word for "seventy times" is *hebdomekontakis*, and it means "countless times." This may seem impossible, and it is in your own strength, but when the Holy Spirit has control of you, then it becomes easier. When I'm having trouble forgiving Larry for forgetting what hours I work, all I have to do is remember how many times I've gone to Jesus asking for forgiveness for the same offense. I'm so thankful that his mercy is continually extended to me, and I draw on his strength to forgive my husband again.

DOES FORGIVENESS EQUAL FORGETTING?

Forgiveness does not equal forgetting. One response I often hear from wives is that they could never forgive because they can't forget what their husbands did. The truth is you probably will remember. God gave you a brain. Part of its job is to remember. The key is not to dwell on the offense. When you find yourself thinking about something negative, stop and begin thinking about something positive. Recently I've started using the phrase "Satan, get behind me." I have found this helpful in stopping those debilitating thoughts. It's funny, but now that I'm writing this book I'm having difficulty remembering the things that my husband "did" to me. Offenses that I thought at the time were worth divorcing him over.

WHAT DO YOU DO NEXT?

Okay, you've decided to forgive your husband. Does this mean bringing out the list and going over each item one by one and asking yourself if you can forgive him for each misdeed? No. I suggest you do something symbolic to represent a complete erasure of your list. You can do it in the privacy of your room or office. You can do it where you're sitting right now. Here are some suggestions that others have told me worked for them:

- Barbara burned a piece of paper as a symbol of destroying her mental list.

- Janet imagined her husband in the chains of her unforgiveness. She symbolically imagined cutting each link, eventually setting him free.

- Phyllis imagined drawing a line in the sand and then stepping over it.

- Larry and I participated in a ceremony where we forgave each other. Perhaps you could arrange this with your pastor.

WHAT IS THE FINAL STEP TO FORGIVENESS?

This may be the toughest step of all. Go to your husband, admit your unforgiving heart, and ask for his forgiveness. Don't say, "I'm sorry." It has probably been overused and at this point means nothing to either of you. Instead ask, "Will you forgive me?" This requires an answer. Go expecting nothing, remembering that your husband is hurting too. He may not trust what you have to say. You might have to give him some time to see the change in you before he's ready to give you an answer. That's okay. This is tough stuff and you've both hurt each other. It may take time, but your marriage is worth it.

I use this lesson almost every day with my friends, children, the guy who just cut me off in traffic, and the store clerk who's being rude to me. Most important, I use it with my husband. He has changed since those bad days, but you know something? He's still not perfect. He never will be perfect, but neither will I. The greatest gift I can give is to accept him as he is, just as God accepts me and loves me anyway.

Living like this is not easy. I extend forgiveness when I have every right to retaliate. I give it because I know it's good for me. I give it because of what Jesus did for me on the cross. He forgave me when I didn't deserve it. One way I can repay him is to forgive my husband, even though he might not deserve it.

The result of living like this? I still get hurt, but I can see myself becoming the person I want to be. I plan to sit in a wheelchair someday dispensing love to everyone around me out of a heart that is full of gratitude.

❧

Action item: Write out a specific plan to symbolically forgive your husband. Review the list of suggestions on page 47 or create your own. Set a specific time and carry out your plan as soon as possible.

CHAPTER SIX

I Can't Change Who I Am

And yet, LORD, you are our Father. We are the clay,
and you are the potter. We are all formed by your hand.
ISAIAH 64:8, NLT

While studying for a degree in food and nutrition, I learned some interesting things about weight loss. By the time you are six years old, your eating habits have been established. That's why when you're thirty-six and trying to lose a few pounds, it's so difficult. You're trying to break a habit that's thirty years old. This is further complicated by the fact that food takes on other roles in our lives. It's not only sustenance, but food comforts us when we're sad, gives us something to do when we're bored, and helps us celebrate almost every happy occasion. We often eat not because we're hungry, but because:

1. It's mealtime.

2. It looks good or tastes good.

3. We feel guilty if we don't clean our plates.

4. We're too polite to turn down dessert.

5. We're using food for entertainment.

6. We think it's a shame that anything goes to waste, so we clean up our children's plates or that last bite of casserole, in essence using ourselves as garbage disposals.

7. We sample as we cook.

8. It temporarily settles our worried, upset stomachs.

9. Food provides momentary peace.

10. It's a way of giving to ourselves when we're denied other pleasures.

Why we eat and when we eat is a complex mixture of physical and psychological needs. No wonder the most successful weight loss programs in America can only boast a 5 percent success rate.[1] Losing weight and keeping it off is a complex process, as are many other changes we try to make in our lives.

Psychologists and theologians spend their lives helping people change. Thousands of self-help books are published every year. They announce that if you subscribe to their method you can lose weight, gain friends, earn more money, get the promotion you want, have a happier marriage, raise good kids, and on and on. They claim to have the answers. Change is individual and is motivated by all sorts of deep psychological and spiritual needs. If change were simple we would all be at our ideal weights, we'd all be happy, and we'd all be rich. Here are some observations I've made over the past few years about the process of making changes.

Step One: Recognize the need to change.
After six years of marriage, we bought a house. Larry's job with a local department store paid well enough that when our first son was born, I was able to quit my job as a school dietitian and be a full-

time mom. We started attending church; Larry became a Christian and I rededicated my life to Christ. We planted a vegetable garden, and I canned fruits and froze jam. Everything seemed perfect.

Then the bottom dropped out. Larry quit his job to work for a friend, who misrepresented the opportunity he was offering. After one short month, Larry was out of work and I was scared to death. Nothing that we'd experienced before had prepared us to work together through this. I needed reassurance, instead Larry withdrew. I needed him to fix the problem, instead he seemed to make it worse. He refused to listen to my advice and in fact got angry when I offered it. A huge gap opened between us, and as we struggled through the next year it grew wider.

Fear of not being able to pay our bills, losing our home, and having to leave my baby and go back to work filled my waking hours and robbed me of sleep at night. When I got angry, it was because of what Larry had done or said or failed to do. The man I thought I married disappeared and in his place was someone who didn't seem to care. I accused and criticized and then was hurt when he reacted. I let my tone of voice say what I couldn't say with my words. I grew sarcastic. Anger filled my heart and I justified it as righteous indignation. Selfishness kept me from seeing the pain I inflicted trying to get my needs fulfilled. I belittled my husband and talked about him to my friends. Pride kept me from asking for help or admitting that I might be wrong. Lack of faith kept me from turning to God except in a very superficial way. In short, I was acting like the sinner I was, but I couldn't admit it.

Instead I stuffed my sins, like snakes, into a bag that I carried around on my back. There were times when I was convicted to do something about them. But when I looked into that bag, all I saw was a squirming mess. I was so overwhelmed by the enormity of the problem and so repelled by what I had become, I closed the bag and pretended it didn't exist. But it weighed me down. I wanted to be happy; I wanted the peace that God promised; I wanted to be and do everything everyone wanted from me. Most of all I wanted to be loved by my husband. The more I tried to make him understand and love me, the farther he withdrew. My efforts to fix things were disastrous.

I reached out to God, but he seemed distant. Church became an ordeal. Every week my pastor seemed to speak directly to me, stirring that nest of vipers in my sack. I hated to be around happy people; I hated to be around Christians. If they knew who I was, they wouldn't like me very much. My biggest fear during that time was to see the revulsion I felt for myself mirrored in someone else's face.

It took all my courage to finally confide in someone that my perfect marriage was in trouble. The person I chose to tell advised me to shut up, go home, and learn to appreciate what I had. The second person I told was a pastor's wife who dropped by our house. She sympathized, but she never came back. I was embarrassed and ashamed.

And so I turned to the world for answers. I found a full-time job hoping to recapture some of the self-esteem and happiness I'd found at my previous job. I told everyone it was to ease our financial problems, but in the back of my mind I knew it would be a source of income to support the boys and me if things didn't get better. But my job didn't ease anything. It only added to my guilt because now I was leaving my children. Hungry for a bit of attention and acceptance, I began flirting with men at work. I started smoking, feeling happily sinful. I toyed more and more with the idea of leaving. I searched for stories of women who divorced and seemed better off. I told myself my babies were young, they would adjust; kids were flexible, they'd get over it. Meanwhile the glass of wine with dinner turned into a bottle.

The world's way eased my pain temporarily, but leaving my husband would've been like putting a Band-Aid on a cancer. It might have felt good for a while to get out from under the tension that had grown up between us, but in the long run it wouldn't have taken care of my problems. I would've only been exchanging them for a whole set of new ones, and the losers would have been my children, my husband, my friends and family, and me. Before you go the world's way, you need to answer a question: What do you want?

What I wanted more than anything was to love and be loved by my husband. Isn't that every woman's dream—to find her true love and then live happily ever after? The problem was that my way of getting what I wanted wasn't working. My solution? Change the man. God's solution? Change me.

I could've left my husband, but I would've still been left with me. I could've found love in another man, but that relationship would've been destroyed by the same thing that was destroying this one—me. Once I acknowledged that I was an equal part of the problem and that I needed to change as much or more than Larry, my marriage began to heal.

Step Two: Admit that you are a sinner.
Sin has become an old-fashioned word. Our society is into self-esteem and gray areas, not responsibility and black and whites. We're asked to be sympathetic to someone, because of his childhood experiences, who just committed murder. We wink at adultery, saying it's none of our business. Our children are surprised when they get caught shoplifting. After all, isn't everyone doing it?

Even in church sin is a word seldom heard. Instead we talk about being oppressed by evil spirits and tempted by Satan. We flash our knowledge of the Bible and feel proud that we're not like other sinners. We don't steal, commit adultery, or murder. We tithe, we pray, and we attend church on Sunday. Isn't that enough?

Jesus raised the standards. He said it wasn't what was on the outside, but what was on the inside. "There is no creature hidden from His sight, but all things are naked and open to the eyes of Him to whom we must give account."[2] He called the Pharisees hypocrites because they gave a tenth of their spices—mint, dill, and cumin—but neglected the more important matters of the law—justice, mercy, and faithfulness. "You cleanse the outside of the cup and dish, but inside they are full of extortion and self-indulgence."[3] He also said that being angry with our brother was the same as murder and that lusting in our hearts was the same as adultery.[4]

It's not only what we do on the outside, but it's what we think and feel on the inside. Who then is without sin? Not me, that's for sure. There was a time in my life when I knew that. At age eleven my mom decided that my two sisters and I should all be baptized on Easter Sunday. Eleven seems awfully young now, but I knew that was what I wanted to do. I had done things that God, my mom and dad, my grandparents, teachers, and friends would all have considered wrong. I stole money out of my mom's purse; I goaded my older sister into fighting and then acted innocent so she'd get in trouble. You might think these were just childish acts, but there was a side of me that liked doing those things. The other side of me, the side that wanted to be a good little girl, was horrified. I didn't want to be bad; I wanted to be good, but the more I tried to be good, the more I seemed to do bad. I remember once walking to town with the express purpose of shoplifting a candy bar. I stopped at the drugstore, the grocery store, and at a café. At each one I thought about how to do it. I sweated as I watched the people behind the counter for my opportunity. Thankfully, I never got up the nerve. But I remember wanting to do it. At eleven, I knew I didn't measure up and carried a lot of guilt. So when it was explained to me that Jesus would wash away my sins, I wanted to be baptized.

But at twenty-eight, my life in a shambles, it wasn't all that easy to admit I was a sinner. First, I thought that meant I was a failure. Second, I thought that made me unlovable and that the people I loved most would reject me. I had to keep up the facade; to lower it would mean rejection.

Jesus said, "Come to me, all of you who are weary and carry heavy burdens, and I will give you rest."[5] Admitting that I was a sinner was the most freeing moment in my life. I didn't have to pretend anymore. I could admit that I was human. I forgot birthdays, I stumbled over my words, I felt fear and anger. I said things that hurt people. I was thoughtless and often selfish. It was okay.

Perfection had been my goal, and I had thought I could do it in my own power. My sins were many, but they were disguised. Pride and selfishness had blinded me. According to the world's standards, I had accomplished much. I'd graduated from college and had a professional degree in dietetics. My babies were cuter, smarter, and bigger than most. When I recommitted my life to God, I had felt that God was pretty lucky to have me in his kingdom.

I had been like a Pharisee who looked good on the outside but was rotting on the inside. Only I hadn't known it. Restoration and real growth began when I broke before him and admitted I had sinned.

Step Three: Name the sin.

It's not enough to say, "God, forgive my sins." You have to name the sin and recognize how it's hurting the people around you. I've learned to use scripture as a mirror. I've been reading in James, and he says clearly that the tongue is the root of all our evil. When I read that verse, I suddenly became aware of a time when I'd made a sarcastic remark to my supervisor about one of my coworkers who consistently arrived for work late. At that moment I could've said, "God, forgive me for gossiping," and that would've been okay, but it wouldn't have changed me because I didn't ask forgiveness for the real problem. I have to go deeper and recognize the root of why I gossip. I do it because, for a moment, I'm the center of attention. I also do it because it makes me feel superior to someone else. The truth is, it shows the world my unforgiving spirit and lack of love. It hurts not only the person I'm gossiping about, but me too. It's also a terrible witness for Jesus Christ to my coworkers. When I delve deeply into my motive for gossiping, then I'm reaching the core of my problem. I now have some concrete things to ask forgiveness for. If I recognize how this sin is hurting others around me, my repentance can be real. The chance of my truly changing is greater.

Step Four: Lay your sin at Christ's feet and ask him to forgive you.

I repent, committing to change not in my power, but in God's power. I can't do it alone; I can only do it through the Holy Spirit working in me. One of my biggest criticisms of my husband during those bad days was his lack of courage in standing up to me. I thought I wanted someone strong who would say no. Instead he backed down from every fight and let me have my way. He often would lie or do things out of what I judged as fear of me. My respect for him was just about gone. One day, as I read a Christian book, I suddenly saw how my critical attitude was responsible for turning my husband into this person I didn't like. Every time he tried to assert himself, I attacked. I knew his vulnerable places and I used this knowledge to wound him. My responsibility for his behavior was so clear and the damage I'd caused him personally so convicting that I got on my knees and prayed for God's forgiveness.

In Mark there is a story about a paraplegic who needed physical healing. His friends knew about Jesus' reputation for healing, but it was impossible to get through the crowds that pressed around him all the time. So they devised a way to get him in to see Jesus. They cut a hole in the roof of the home where Jesus was speaking and lowered him on a mat. Jesus must have been impressed by the tenacity of this man and his friends. Before Jesus healed this man, he first forgave his sins. He told the crowd that forgiving the man's sins was more of a miracle than the physical healing.[6]

At the moment I asked God's forgiveness for my critical attitude, I experienced a miracle. It was as if a warm hand reached into my aching heart and healed it. I felt whole and clean and humbled by what had taken place. I knew I was forgiven. At that point change began in me from the inside out.

Since that day, I've experienced this touch of forgiveness many times. God is faithful and has continually forgiven me, even when I've gone back time and time again for the same sin. Never think that God tires of your repentance.

God's gracious, unending, and tireless forgiveness is one of his best gifts to each of his children. Instead of beating us down, he frees us.

Step Five: Undergo radical surgery.
Sometimes to avoid sinning we need to make radical changes in our lives. I know of a woman who had a problem with temptation. There was a terrific bakery at the mall where she shopped, and every time she passed it she went in and bought a gooey cinnamon roll. She just couldn't seem to stop herself. She finally got a handle on this problem by going out a back entrance to the mall, thus avoiding the bakery altogether. In the same way, the problem I was experiencing with flirtation at work went away when I changed jobs. Drastic? Yes, but I think this is what Jesus meant when he said in the Sermon on the Mount, "If your right eye causes you to sin, gouge it out and throw it away. It is better for you to lose one part of your body than for your whole body to be thrown into hell."[7] Maybe it's a friend who's feeding your unhappiness in your marriage. End the friendship. Maybe it's your job; perhaps it's what you're reading or watching on television. I stopped watching soap operas and reading romance novels. They fed my unhappiness because they gave me an unrealistic image of what marriage and love were all about.

The following modern fairy tale will illustrate this clearly. Once upon a time there was a royal podiatrist. One day he stubbed his big toe and got a small splinter. It hurt, but not enough to do anything about. He took two aspirin and went about his busy life tending to the royal family. Infection set in, the toe swelled, turned black, and the nail fell off. Slowly the infection crawled up his veins into his leg. At night the pain would be excruciating, but during the day, while he was busy treating his royal patients, he could ignore it. He did all the right things to keep healthy; he exercised daily, ate the right foods, watched his cholesterol, and didn't drink or smoke. However, the infection turned gangrenous and eventually killed him. When he got to heaven he was asked why he hadn't taken care of the problem. He replied, "I am a podiatrist and podiatrists don't have problems with their feet."

The royal podiatrist had access to the latest medical technology; he didn't seek help because he was a doctor. We often don't seek help because we are Christians. And yet we have access to the greatest healer of all, Jesus Christ. Remember what he did for us when we first believed? He came in and wiped away our sins completely. He separated us from our sins: "As far as the east is from the west, so far has He removed our transgressions from us."[8]

When I sin I don't lose my salvation, but I do lose something almost as precious. I lose my intimate relationship with God. I have now experienced God's healing touch many times, and I expect to continue to sense it as I seek to grow. On my knees before God, I found peace, I found happiness, and I found hope.

❧

Action item: Buy or borrow a copy of *The Message* by Eugene Peterson and read Matthew 5, 6, and 7. Pick out one area of your life where you feel guilt. Ponder how this "sin" has affected those around you. When you are ready, ask for God's forgiveness. Let him wash you clean.

CHAPTER SEVEN

I Can't Change the Way I Feel

Take your everyday, ordinary life—your sleeping, eating, going-to-work, and walking-around life—and place it before God as an offering. . . . You'll be changed from the inside out.

ROMANS 12:1–2, *THE MESSAGE*

$\mathcal{T}$he biggest barriers I faced when I decided to stay with my husband and work through our problems were my feelings. I didn't experience those warm fuzzies that I had thought were signs of true love. In fact, what I felt was something closer to antipathy. My mind said "stay" because it was best for everyone, but my feelings screamed "go" because I couldn't be sure that things would get better. Staying meant going against my feelings, the very determinant I had used to guide almost every decision in my life.

When we bought a car, the one I wanted had nothing to do with its cost or how reliable it was but on how I felt about it. When I met someone new, I judged their character on how I felt around them. I bought a dog, not because I could afford it or wanted to take care of it, but because I'd read a book when I was in the fourth grade about a cocker spaniel and it stirred a strong emotional response within me. I even chose a career, not on the basis of what I wanted to do for the rest of my life, but on how it would feel to be a professional dietitian—only one of a few in the United States.

Now these weren't all bad decisions. Some of them even turned out well. But some of my decisions were disasters. I spent five years training to be a dietitian, but didn't actually like being one. I also have an old cocker spaniel that wakes me up in the early morning scratching on the door, requires expensive grooming, and has multiple health problems that are weaknesses in her breed.

My emotions can be an asset, but they can also lead me into making some major mistakes. I can't live my life based solely on how I feel about things. Otherwise I wouldn't go to work, do housework, shop for groceries, weed the garden, or any of a myriad of things that I find tedious. We do lots of things we don't feel like doing because they are good for us or good for our family or because they're the right things to do or because doing the hard work now will lead to another reward later (like a paycheck). I'm sitting here at my computer right now typing away on this manuscript, and it's a beautiful spring day. My feelings say, *Go outside,* but my mind says, *No, you must stay with this if you're ever going to finish the book.* Following your feelings is fraught with potential pitfalls. Dr. James Dobson in his book *Emotions: Can You Trust Them?* says, "[Emotion] has a definite place in human affairs, but when forced to stand alone, feelings usually reveal themselves to be unreliable and ephemeral and even a bit foolish."[1]

When I was in the middle of my marital problems, I was a walking, breathing mass of feelings, most of them negative. I was angry, full of guilt, lonely, unloved, embarrassed, and ashamed. These were all mixed up inside me like a boiling cauldron of oil. When I couldn't deal with them any longer, I tried asking Larry to help me sort them out, but this only seemed to make him angry and confused me more. Counseling didn't help and reading the Bible only seemed to make me feel worse. Nothing seemed to help. I tried covering this mass of darkness with busyness, alcohol, food, sleep, long baths, movies, and books—anything that would ease the pain for a while. But these were just escapes and as such just Band-Aids for the real problems. The good feelings I experienced were rare and often short-lived as things spiraled downward.

One of the important steps to healing my marriage and myself began when I finally learned to deal with that black, ugly cauldron of emotions. My understanding was deepened when I took the time to really examine the role feelings are designed to play in my life.

FEELINGS ARE INNER RESPONSES TO OUTER STIMULI

Feelings are inner responses to outer stimuli. Examples of physical reactions are: If I touch something hot, I feel pain. If I eat something sweet, I feel pleasure. If I smell home-baked bread, I feel hungry. Emotional responses to outside stimuli include: If I see something I consider sad, I cry. If someone says something I think is an insult, I get angry. We all react differently to emotional stimuli. Hallmark commercials make me cry. My son sitting next to me watching the same commercial may laugh because he sees it for what it is—an ad that is aimed at convincing me to buy a certain brand of greeting card. He's reacting one way; I'm reacting another.

What makes me happy may not affect another person at all. I'm particularly emotional over daffodils and lilacs. They remind me of my childhood and especially of my grandmother. These are happy memories for me, but what if I'd had a particularly painful childhood or a mean, hateful grandmother? Then I would feel differently, wouldn't I?

YOU CATCH A COLD, NOT FEELINGS

If our feelings are indeed responses that come from within, then this means that our husbands don't give them to us. I can't count the number of times I've accused my husband of making me feel unloved, angry, hurt, ashamed, or embarrassed. But the truth is, I did all of those things to myself. He might have stimulated the feeling by a remark, but the feeling itself was just an inner response.

Sometimes it truly does seem that my husband makes me feel angry, because he knows my hot buttons. But the truth remains, it's our reaction coming from inside us. You can choose not to react.

For example, when Larry and I travel together, we often get angry with each other. Why? Because he follows the car in front of us too closely. I've told him many times how uncomfortable this makes me, but he still does it. My feeling is anger. In fact what I'm doing is making a judgment about his motive. I think he's being uncaring. In reality, that's not his motive at all. To him he's not following too close. He considers the distance between the two cars safe. I don't. I could say he's making me feel angry, but in reality it's my fear that's causing me to feel this way, not him.

GOD CREATED OUR FEELINGS, EVEN THE BAD ONES

We were created in God's image, and feelings and emotions are something we share in common with him. If you read the Bible you'll see that Jesus cried, got angry, became frustrated with his disciples, loved, and felt joy. Emotions help us live life fully. Without them life would be pretty dull. Love makes us good mothers, grandmothers, wives, and friends. Joy helps me appreciate the simple grace of a chickadee feeding at my birdfeeder in the morning, the warmth of a spring day, and the colors of the rainbow reflected in the raindrops on my rhododendrons. Guilt is a good barometer for sin in my life. Dissatisfaction and unhappiness can lead us to seek the Lord. Peace is the reward for fully accepting Jesus as our Lord and Savior. When we get off track, often it's our feelings that bring us back. Anger can lead us to write a letter to the editor that can share the truth with a large number of readers or stand up for what is right at our workplace. It's important to realize that our feelings are intended to be life-enhancers.

God even speaks to us through our emotions. For seven years I taught creative writing at a local technical college. I loved teaching and thought I'd probably do it the rest of my life. Slowly, I began to resent the time it was taking to critique all those manuscripts. I ignored the feeling at first, believing I was just tired, but it persisted. Through prayer I began to believe this was God's way of telling me it was time to move on. The very next quarter I had students who handed in objectionable material, something that I had not faced before. I discussed the decision with my husband and with several godly friends. Their feedback confirmed my decision to leave. Something I never thought I'd do.

Overall, emotions are a good thing. It's only when they get out of control that they cause trouble.

FEELINGS ARE NEITHER GOOD NOR BAD, THEY JUST ARE

That's easy to say when we're talking about "good" feelings like happiness, joy, and peace. But we don't feel the same way about anger, frustration, or sadness. We assign value to them. They are "bad."

But if Jesus felt them, how can they be bad? They aren't, but what we do with our emotions can be wrong. Feeling angry in itself is not a sin; however, when you strike out with your hand or your words and hurt someone, then it becomes a sin.

You only have to read a few psalms to realize they are full of deep emotions and not all of them good. In Psalm 69 David cries out, "Save me, O God, for the waters have come up to my neck. I sink in the miry depths, where there is no foothold. I have come into the deep waters; the floods engulf me. I am worn out calling for help; my throat is parched."[2] Doesn't that sound like someone drowning in misery and begging God for a way out?

FEELINGS COME FROM OUR BELIEFS

Christian psychologist Larry Crabb says feelings radiate out of what we believe about ourselves. It's because of this that they can seem irrational. Sometimes it's obvious why we feel the way we do. If we're called a fat pig, we rise up in anger because we are insulted. When someone hands us a bouquet of flowers and says I love you, we respond with warm feelings. These are rational reactions. But sometimes our reactions are not that simple. When insulted we may react by laughing. A gift may end up making us angry. Our reaction is determined by what we believe about ourselves and the motive behind the action.

If we believe that we are beautiful and someone calls us a fat pig, it might make us laugh, or we might even ignore it. But if we believe we are ugly and hate the fact that we're twenty pounds overweight and have been struggling all our lives to lose a few pounds, then when someone calls us a fat pig, it wounds us deeply. It touches the very core of what we believe about ourselves.

Remember the greeting cards my husband showered me with? To a casual observer, sending the cards appeared to be a thoughtful, loving act. And they were at first. But when his actions didn't back up the words on the cards, they became a mockery of my feelings. I wanted warm, loving arms and a listening ear and thoughtful acts, not someone else's words on beautiful paper surrounded by lovely artwork. I responded out of a belief that he didn't love me.

In Stormie Omartian's autobiography she tells about coming

home late from work and finding a rose on her door. At first she was flattered by the attention, but then as the roses continued to arrive daily over the next fourteen nights, Stormie became afraid. She found the flower gifts to be unsettling and frightening. Her fear was exacerbated by the Sharon Tate murders just a few miles from where she lived. The rose became a thing of terror. She responded out of a belief that there was someone dangerous behind those flowers.

If I believe I am loved by my husband, when he forgets Valentine's Day, it's easy to shrug it off as just human frailty. If on the other hand, I'm worried that he doesn't love me, it can be the proof I was looking for to confirm what I feared most.

I think you can see now that the key to understanding our feelings lies in discovering the underlying beliefs we hold about ourselves. These beliefs are planted in our formative years by our parents, teachers, friends, books we read, and things we experience. The beliefs may be true or false. They can be positive or negative.

Here is a list of beliefs I carry around with me:

- If I do everything right, then I will be loved.
- My hard work will be rewarded.
- Thin people are more acceptable than fat people.
- People who do special things, like write books, star in plays, sing solos at church, or win Olympic medals, are loved more.
- People who show their anger are bad.
- When I find my "true love," then I will be happy.
- If I don't agree with my friends, they won't like me.
- I am responsible for my husband's happiness.
- The key to happiness is having lots of people love you.
- I can make my children happy.

What do you believe about yourself? You might want to create your own list. Do you think you're pretty, or do you see yourself as ugly and unacceptable?

The first time I met my friend, whom I will call Elizabeth, I thought she was the most beautiful woman I'd ever seen. She was tall and slender and had thick, long blond hair. She looked like a model. When I told her this, she laughed and said, "When I look in the mirror all I see is my ugly nose. As a child, I was called Witch Hazel by most of the kids in school." I wondered if she'd had a great plastic surgeon or had been an ugly duckling that had grown into a real beauty. Then she showed me. There was a small bump on her nose that I hadn't even noticed. To her it was huge and the only thing she saw when she looked into the mirror. I saw the complete person, and to me she was truly beautiful.

That encounter made me realize that I did the same thing. I couldn't see the real me either, because I was tuned in to my physical defects, or at least what I considered defects. When I look in the mirror I see a chin that sticks out funny (my cousins teased me mercilessly about my hangy-down chin), thin lips (full lips are now all the rage), and a fuzz of hair over my lip. When I was fourteen or fifteen, I decided to read *War and Peace*. I was doing pretty well until I got to the place where a woman was described as ugly and unacceptable because she had a mustache. A warm flush of embarrassment and shame washed over me as I realized I had a mustache. I had never even noticed it before then, but after I read that statement it was like a neon light surrounded my upper lip. I bleached it. One of the boys commented. I shaved it off, but it felt unnatural and when it grew back, it was bristly. Probably if you met me, you wouldn't even notice this perceived flaw. But I'm self-conscious about it even today. (I put down *War and Peace*, and to this day I cannot bring myself to read it.)

Seeing the real you and finding out why you react the way you do to outer stimuli can take a lot of prayer and soul-searching. The next time you react out of proportion to the situation, try doing the following things:

1. *Examine your motives.*

Step back and remove yourself from the situation and look for what's going on. I found that writing for a few minutes helped me clarify my thoughts. Search your childhood, especially your vulnerable adolescence; listen to the voices in your head. Seek the truth about yourself. Instead of denying that you're feeling something negative, make friends with it.

2. *Name the feeling(s).*

This may sound simple, but if you're looking into a black cauldron of emotions right now, it may be hard. It was particularly hard for me to admit that I carried all of those negative feelings around inside of me, but it was a relief when I wrote the words down: anger, resentment, bitterness, jealousy, envy, to name a few.

3. *Look for the root feeling(s).*

Fear, embarrassment, guilt, and shame are often the first responses to anger. "What am I feeling right now?" is a good question and not always easy to answer. We may be feeling angry, but what triggered that response may be something else entirely. Yesterday morning I woke up feeling depressed and angry for no apparent reason. I went downstairs, got the paper, poured myself a cup of coffee, and sat at the table. Larry, as usual, fixed our breakfast. As he bustled around the kitchen, I found myself being irritated at him. His conversation seemed shallow, and I resented the fact that I couldn't read an important article in the paper. I bit my tongue and wished he'd just leave for work. It took everything I had to keep from jumping all over him.

After he left, I had my quiet time and I realized what was going on. I was overwhelmed by the sin I was facing in the world around me. At work there was a man who came into the library and brought up pornography on the Internet in full view of children. I had been told there was nothing I could do about it. A well-known politician had been accused of adultery, and everyone around me was dismissing the sin as normal behavior. It was his business what he did in his personal life. Someone I admired had been accused of sexual misconduct, and I didn't know if he was innocent or guilty.

My irritation was coming from an overwhelming sense of helplessness. If I'd followed my first feeling, I would've yelled at my husband and we would've left for work feeling angry with each other.

These three steps, examining my motives, naming the feeling, and finding the root cause have become helpful tools. I'm able to see the real issues behind my feelings, which enables me to do something about them.

For example, I don't like working in the garden, but every once in a while I get the urge to dig in the dirt. I remember one afternoon being restless and since it was a beautiful spring day, I went outside. I pulled a few weeds here and there, and before I knew it I'd cleaned up most of the front garden. When I looked at my handiwork, I said, "This is good. I could enjoy gardening." And so I made plans to buy some plants and came up with an idea for a bare spot by the mailbox. I could hardly wait for Larry to get home; he was going to be so proud of me. And he was, until I got to the part about my plans. He does most of the yard work and is somewhat of an expert on what makes things grow. He told me why my idea wouldn't work.

I was hurt and angry, overly so. After I calmed down I stepped back from the situation and asked myself, Okay, what is going on here? Why did I overreact to his comments? He didn't mean them to be hurtful, but they injured me deeply. Then I realized that I was feeling like the little sister again. I grew up with a big sister. She was good at everything and thought it was her job to teach me. My ideas were never good enough. She was always undoing things I'd done and doing them over the right way. When Larry questioned my idea, he raised in me old specters that had nothing at all to do with the situation.

Getting in touch with these deep beliefs can be difficult but can lead to a more fulfilling life. For one thing, you can decide if they are true. My belief that people who are stupid just don't measure up to the world's standard, and the deep fear that I may appear that way has handicapped me in many ways. For example, I struggle for days with a new computer program trying to figure it out myself, when a phone call to a tech service would solve the problem in minutes. At work my boss may give me directions that I don't quite understand, but out of fear of appearing stupid, I won't ask for clarification, which leads me into making mistakes. In groups such as Sunday school, Bible study, and classes, I often don't ask questions or state my opinion because I'm afraid.

The truth is, I'm not stupid. I have a good mind and often what I have to say is worthwhile and the question I want to ask is just the question that the rest of the people in the group are wondering too. But the voice that whispers that I'm stupid is incredibly strong. I fight it almost every day of my life. The question I need to ask is, So what? Where in the Bible does it say only the smart will enter heaven? I think it's interesting that it says the opposite. It says the things of God are foolishness to the world.

Become an Actor, Not a Reactor

One of the fruits of the Spirit is self-control. This means acting purposefully, not just reacting to your feelings. When I got in touch with my feelings and understood where they came from, I became an actor in my life, not a reactor. An actor does what she wants to do based on facts; a reactor becomes a victim and is swayed by her circumstances and the people around her. She's afraid of what others might think and measures everything she does by this ruler.

After realizing this, I spoke up in groups and asked the questions that needed answers, even though I was afraid of appearing stupid. I took a writing class, even though I thought I had no talent. I stopped feeling guilty when my husband became angry or looked sad or withdrew into the garage. This allowed me to stay cool during arguments.

Last night on the news I heard an aspiring actor say that to be successful he had to overcome the fear of making a fool of himself. I think this is good advice for all of us. One of my greatest fears was speaking in front of groups. In the past few years I have developed this unexplainable desire to do just that. Now I look for these opportunities and I enjoy it.

I've gotten that black cauldron of boiling emotion under control and it has freed me. Oh sure, I still get angry and have what I call black days, but they're no longer the devastating events that they used to be. I've learned not to panic and that if I wait my mood will lift.

Don't Blame Others for Your Feelings

If my bad feelings don't come from Larry, then neither do my good feelings. When I was down, I used to think that it was my husband's responsibility to make me feel better. But no one can make me feel better, only I can do that. If you've been living like a victim, it might be hard to know what makes you happy. It might take some exploration. Try doing something nice for yourself every day. Maybe you were doing some of these things earlier as Band-Aids to cover up your negative feelings. Now you are going to put on a new attitude. You are going to start doing things to make yourself happy. Take a walk in a local park, buy a latte, splurge on flowers, take a long bath, read a good book, go to the library, visit an art museum, sit in the sun, call a friend and go out to lunch.

You might believe that doing something nice for yourself is selfish, but it's not. You are doing it for your marriage, for your children, for your friends. Who wants to be around someone who's depressed all the time? No one. One of the sweetest things you can say to your husband is, "I feel happy right now."

TRUST GOD, NOT YOUR FEELINGS

Don't wait for your feelings to tell you to do the right thing. Do the right thing, and then your feelings will follow. I stayed with my husband, not because I felt like it, but because it was what God wanted me to do. Do you suppose Jesus felt like going to the cross? He did it because he was obedient. He did it because he loves us. Many years ago I placed myself in God's hands. I decided to trust him, and I'm glad I did.

"Trust and obey, for there's no other way to be happy in Jesus, but to trust and obey."[3]

Whom are you going to trust? God or your feelings? You have to make the choice.

❧

Action item: List seven inexpensive things you consider a luxury and then do one of them for yourself every day for the next week.

CHAPTER EIGHT

I Had So Many Dreams

*Much marriage difficulty and unhappiness are due to the failure
of the partners to accept the fact of their finiteness and its
meaning. Instead, they hold themselves up to ideals of
performance possible only to God.*

REUL HOWE[1]

$\mathcal{T}$here once was a playwright who wrote a script for two lovers.
The setting was romantic, the dialogue fascinating, and the action
compelling. When it came time to act out the scene, the playwright decided she would take the major role. The other actor
entered from the right and waited for his lines. The playwright
spoke the first line, paused, and waited for the other actor to
respond. The other actor said what he thought was an intelligent
response. The playwright glared and then spoke another line. The
actor tried, but everything he did or said only made the playwright
angry. The playwright finally threw the script on the ground,
called the actor stupid, and fired him immediately.

When the actor was asked why he failed he said, "She never gave me my lines."

Unreasonable? Yes, but don't we do this to our husbands? Larry and I were married six years before we had children. One of our favorite things was dining out at fine restaurants in the area. We would linger over dessert and coffee and have long conversations about all sorts of things. But when our children came along things changed.

A night out became a big event. One year for my birthday, we made plans to go to my favorite restaurant. I looked forward to it all day. I planned what I'd wear, imagined what I'd order (pan-fried oysters), and thought about how romantic it was going to be, just the two of us. We'd have one of our deep conversations like we used to have. Larry would make me laugh and look into my eyes and listen to what I said. Afterward we'd take a casual walk along the streets of our small tourist town looking into the windows of all the quaint shops.

As I bathed and dressed in my black dress, the one that Larry especially liked, I thought about how nothing was going to get in the way of the evening. It was going to be a new beginning. After months of tension and quarreling, we were going to recapture some of the closeness we'd known before.

Thankfully, my dress still fit even though I'd gained some weight, but the only pair of shoes that matched were my spike heels and they hurt my feet. We dropped the boys off at my sister's, but just before we left, David threw up on me. The restaurant was crowded and we could hardly hear each other and they were out of pan-fried oysters. Larry was tired and after discussing what to order we ran out of conversation. I asked about his day, but didn't want to hear the same old complaints. I wanted to talk about more important things like our dreams for the future, our love for one another, something deep and meaningful. Instead we talked about kids and, believe it or not, the weather. I looked at the stranger across the table and hated the boring couple we'd become.

Why couldn't he try a little harder? Why couldn't we talk like we used to? Was this the way we were going to be for the rest of our lives? Disappointment and anger swelled inside of me.

When he suggested we look in the shop windows, I told him my feet hurt and not in a tone of voice that anyone would call sweet. We drove home. The distance between us was now greater than before.

I wanted to blame Larry for the disastrous evening, and part of the blame did rest on him. But part of it, and maybe even most of it, rested on me. Just like the playwright, I'd set up the evening for failure. I'd written a script and when Larry didn't follow it, I was angry and disappointed. This is called an unrealistic expectation.

An unrealistic expectation is putting our hope for happiness on the things and people of this world. I will be happy if the evening goes as I planned. I will be happy if my husband picks up his socks. I will be happy when we buy a house. All of these things have one thing in common—they are out of my control.

I couldn't keep the baby from throwing up. I couldn't make Larry rested. I couldn't control whether or not the restaurant had pan-fried oysters. I could control what I wore and what I talked about and how I treated my husband. Maybe if I'd been more attentive and caring about his work problem, he would've been more interested in my problems. We can't control what other people do or say. We can't control the weather or traffic or many of our circumstances. We can't make a friend call us. We can't make our children be what we want them to be. Thinking we can will lead to a lifetime of disappointment.

THE SOURCE OF UNREALISTIC EXPECTATIONS

So where do these unrealistic expectations come from? The answer is as individual as we are.

Past experiences. One of my biggest mistakes is trying to recapture something that happened in the past. I'll remember a time when we were particularly close and think that if we do whatever it was that made us happy, we'll get the feelings back. The problem with past experiences is we often sugarcoat them so that the reality gets distorted. We forget that the weather was perfect, and we both were rested and feeling particularly close before we even went on the excursion.

Our parents and their marriage. One of my memories of my parents growing up is of them sitting at the kitchen table talking. Dad would come home from work, and they'd sit there laughing and talking while we waited in the other room for dinner. I felt warm and protected as I listened to them discuss the day's events. That was how I thought Larry and I should do things. But when Larry comes home he is hungry and wants to eat immediately. There's no time for talk, and this has left me disappointed.

Perhaps your father was a handyman and did all the repairs around the house, but your husband is all thumbs and doesn't know how to hold a hammer. Your dad brought home little treats, turning an ordinary day into something special; your husband never thinks about things like that. Your dad opened the car door, helped your mother into her coat, and made a big deal of birthdays. Can you see how this can set you up to expect these same sorts of things from your husband?

Books/magazine articles. Books have been my warm companions since I was ten years old. When I was thirteen I read *Gone with the Wind.* It was not unusual for me to stay up all night reading. I learned many good things from these friends, but I also absorbed some things that set me up for disappointment. They filled my head with romantic notions. The hero might not have done the right thing by the heroine in the beginning, but by the end of the book, everything fell neatly into place. He said and did exactly the right thing. This made me think that this was possible in real life. I didn't realize that the author had complete control of every character, while we have no control over anyone except ourselves.

Nonfiction articles and books about marriage can also give us unrealistic expectations. When we began experiencing problems, I read every book I could and would underline the parts that pertained to Larry. Then I would give the book to Larry to read, hoping he'd see all the things he needed to correct. I wanted him to communicate in the way the book said. I wanted him to be romantic. I wanted him to be strong and yet gentle. When he didn't deliver, I was even more disappointed.

Movies/television. I don't think there is anything more damaging than movies and television. A television program may show a couple having problems, but that problem is neatly resolved in an hour and everyone lives happily ever after. Everyone looks beautiful; everyone says his or her lines perfectly, all without ever messing up the house. Life just isn't that neat and tidy. Life is a mess. Often we live with the same frustrations day in and day out. Things sometimes never get resolved. My husband hasn't been given a script so that he knows the right thing to say. And yet I expected him to behave the same way that the screen stars did.

The book and then follow-up movie *Bridges of Madison County* is a good example. In that story a farm wife meets a world-traveling photographer and falls in love. They have a torrid love affair that lasts for three days while her husband and children are attending the state fair. She carries this "love" with her the rest of her life, and upon her death her children learn about him. It's all wonderful and romantic, but anyone can be perfect for three days. I often wonder if she'd run off with him, a loner who lived out of a suitcase, how long it would've been before she woke up and saw the reality of what he was. He lived in a shack. He had no friends. He couldn't stand to be in any one place for very long. It's easy to love a man for three days; it takes guts to love a man when you live with him day in and day out and get to know all of his flaws in an intimate way.

Our friends. My sister told me her husband gave her flowers for Valentine's Day. Not only did he send her one bouquet, but, in order to surprise her, he sent her two because he knew she wouldn't be expecting the second one. When she told me, I was envious. My husband gave me a card and a $2.99 box of chocolates. Other friends go to Hawaii or Mexico or Europe on their vacations. We go to my parents' home in Idaho. Another husband has created a backyard that looks like something out of *Sunset* magazine. Our yard looks a lot more "natural." It's easy to look at other couples and be envious of their relationships. They look so good from the outside looking in.

I'll never forget a couple I met on a Marriage Encounter weekend. They were gorgeous. Both blond, thin, and professionals. They reeked of money. Saturday at noon they approached my husband and me and said they were leaving. They weren't getting much out of the weekend because they already had such a good marriage. Besides, they had a tennis date. I remember being so envious of them as they drove away in their Mercedes. The perfect couple, I thought. A few months later, he left her for another woman.

The church. We are told from the pulpit that our husbands should be the spiritual leaders of our home. I often wonder how many of us go home from that sermon expecting great changes in our men. We want them to begin tithing, to lead us in a regular prayer time, to organize family nights and devotions, and to be in the Bible daily. The reason? The pastor just told us that when they become the spiritual leaders, they will be better husbands. Then we wives will feel loved and honored. Once they get into the Word, they will miraculously turn into the man we've always wanted them to be.

Bonnie told me that after her husband accepted the Lord he turned into a different person. He became much more thoughtful and caring and helped her around the house where before he had been distant and uninvolved with the family. I looked at my husband and wondered why I couldn't tell any difference.

Someone else's expectations. We often try to take on other people's expectations as our own. When we are children, we pick up all sorts of impressions when we hear people talking about other people.

"Sally is a lousy mom. She just lets her kids run wild."

"That Betty, have you seen how fat she is?"

"Have you seen the mess that Mary's house is?"

"She married Bob and he's just a farmer. Won't amount to much."

Subtle messages, but often we take them to heart and vow we'll never be like that. We'll be thin, keep a neat house, marry a man of means, and be a good mom.

If you are a stay-at-home mom, you hear the message that you're wasting your life because you don't work out of the home. It sounds glamorous to be part of an exciting career that involves lots of travel, and we begin to think that happiness must lie there. On the other hand if you're a working mother, you hear the message that you are failing your children if you aren't staying home. What other people are doing always seems so much better than what we're doing. We see the reality of our situation. We often don't see the reality of someone else's situation.

UNREALISTIC EXPECTATIONS OF SELF

On top of these unrealistic expectations for others, we often have them of ourselves. One of my first jobs as a dietitian was at the most highly regarded food service in Seattle. When they hired me, my sons were three and one. My boss made it clear that I was a test; no one was sure I could handle a job and two babies. I took the challenge and vowed I would be the best employee they ever had. I also would take care of my children and keep a perfect house. I could do it. I was young (twenty-eight); I had lots of energy. I would show them they had not made a mistake.

And I did it, for a while. I balanced all of my responsibilities and felt good about the job I was doing. I cooked and cleaned and spent quality time with my children, and I never missed a day of work or complained about the long hours I put in. But after a few months, I was totally exhausted. There were many days I went home crying because I had let someone down, forgotten to be someplace important, had to tell someone no, or wasn't there when one of my sons was sick. I got behind in my housework, often racing out the door with dishes on the counter, something I had vowed never to do. On Saturday I felt as if lead weights were tied to my feet. Every chore seemed like a mountain that needed to be climbed. There just wasn't enough of me to go around. I felt guilty at work; I felt guilty at home.

I wasn't living up to my expectations of myself, and I was miserable. I think a lot of us suffer from the Superwoman image. We have to learn our limitations and accept our human frailties.

LOVE TESTS

Another harmful thing we do is "love tests." If he only did _____, then I'd know he loved me. Women don't like to admit doing this, but unfortunately we're guilty of subjecting our husbands to these tests with no warning. This is particularly damaging because, like the playwright, we're not playing fair. We're not giving our husbands their lines. If he loved me, he'd know how much flowers meant and he'd give them to me on Valentine's Day. If he loved me, he'd be able to read my mind and know that something is bothering me.

One day a woman complained to me about her husband leaving the toilet seat up. By the time we talked, this had become much more than a simple thoughtless act. It had become a symbol of his lack of love and respect for her. "If he loved me, he'd be more thoughtful and put the toilet seat down," she said. "He knows how much this irritates me." She believed that everything her husband did was tied to their relationship. Leaving the seat up had become proof that he didn't love her. The reality may have been that he was just one of those men who truly doesn't think about those things. I doubt very much that he was consciously leaving the seat up and then thinking, "There. That'll show her how I feel." The sooner my friend accepted the fact that her husband was just messy and learned to laugh about his idiosyncrasies, the happier she was going to be.

"Love tests" don't prove a thing. They just make us miserable.

WHAT TO DO ABOUT UNREALISTIC EXPECTATIONS

So how do we stop this damaging behavior? Simply put, I don't think we can ever stop having unrealistic expectations. It's part of our sin nature to want to find our own self-absorbed happiness in the world. I think as we mature as Christians we can get a better handle on our unrealistic expectations, but more than likely we'll never eradicate them entirely.

A letter appeared in Ann Landers's column that sums up what a lot of women today are feeling.

> Dear Ann,
> "Timmy" and I have always gotten along well. We have four terrific kids. I made it a point to teach our children that Daddy comes first. He is king in our house. They love him and respect him. He is a wonderful father. But there must be more to life than PTA, housework, cooking, cleaning, laundry, and sex with your husband. I ache to feel that special electricity when my eyes meet those of a handsome man across a crowded room. It never happens. I yearn for a lover who will make my heart pound a mile a minute. Timmy used to—but the thrill is gone. Things are quiet, calm and—I might as well say it—dull as dishwater. We have a lot

to be thankful for—good health, attractive, well-behaved kids, and a promising financial future. Why isn't this enough? Is something wrong with me? Am I chasing the impossible dream?

Moonglow.

This is how Ann replied:

Put away your storybooks, little girl. You've got some growing up to do. Yes, there is more to life than PTA, housework, cooking, cleaning, laundry, and sex with your husband. There's illness, infidelity, and emotional breakdowns that make it impossible for some women to do the housework, cooking, cleaning, and laundry. As for sex with your husband, don't knock it, honey. There are plenty of husbands who aren't interested and an equal number who are getting sex someplace else. There is also alcoholism, in-law trouble, out-of-control children, unemployment, and money worries. Read the papers. Look around. Case your friends. No marriage can maintain the full-moon-June-honeymoon level of excitement forever. And it's a good thing. We would all collapse from exhaustion. Time diminishes the raging fires to a soft glow—present, but no longer ferocious and demanding. Count your blessings. Too many people fail to appreciate what they have until they have lost it. Don't let this happen to you.[2]

Learn to recognize unrealistic expectations. Whenever you find yourself upset, find some time to be alone with the Lord. Some of my best insights into my own behavior have come after reading the Scriptures and praying openly and honestly to God: "Why did I get so upset? Why did I react that way? Help me understand, Lord." Once you've identified the source, then you can do something about it.

A woman in my Bible study told of her greatest frustration. Every evening she would fix a nice dinner for her husband and three teenagers. She would put a lot of time and planning into the preparation and looked forward to the whole family sitting around the table, enjoying her food and one another's company. The reality was her three children were normal, busy teenagers with all sorts of school activities. Rarely were they even home for dinner, and if they were they wolfed it down and raced out the door without thanking her. This upset her. She thought they were disrespectful and thoughtless. She was upset with them and angry with her husband because he didn't make them eat her dinner. Almost every evening was ruined for her—and by her.

She cooked her meals freely; no one asked her to do it. She gave a gift and then expected to receive praise and glory. The scripture says, "If you lend to those from whom you expect repayment, what credit is that to you? Even 'sinners' lend to 'sinners,' expecting to be repaid in full. But love your [family], do good to them, and lend to them without expecting to get anything back. Then your reward will be great, and you will be sons of the Most High, because he is kind to the ungrateful and wicked" (Luke 6:34–35).

She can address her problem by simply letting go of the idea of a "big dinner" every night. She could make one night a week the "main meal," perhaps Sunday or Monday. Then everyone would know that they were expected to be there for it, or she could simply just accept the fact that her family is changing and things won't be as she wants them.

Live with an open hand. A man recently told me he was going away with his wife for the weekend. After I made some remark about how wonderful that sounded, he just shook his head. "These weekends never turn out the way I want. I actually dread them."

I knew exactly what he was saying. How many times have Larry and I gone away with a bag packed with our clothes and our unrealistic expectations? Larry sees these weekends as a chance for some sexual play and an opportunity to poke around in a local museum and discover something of interest about the town we are going to visit. He sees us getting up early and hiking along the beach.

I see them as times when we'll draw closer together and talk about the things that are bothering us. I expect to recapture some of the feelings that have gotten lost in the busyness of our lives. I want to sleep in as late as possible, read a good book, and maybe catch a movie.

I go with one agenda, Larry with another. And they often clash. Instead of the romantic weekend I visualized, we snap at each other and come home disappointed.

Through years of trial and error I've discovered a better way. Go with an open hand. We've learned to pull the car over to the side of the road and say, Okay, what do you want out of this time away? Instead of setting an agenda, we discuss our expectations and then go with the attitude of let's see what happens. We both try to accommodate the other's wishes, without feeling imprisoned by our mate's expectations.

Accept your husband for who he is. I know a couple who sat down and made a list of all the things she wanted him to do around the house and then prioritized it. She saw this as a solution to getting all those odd jobs done around the house. Instead, when he didn't complete the projects in a timely manner, the list became a weapon. She was disappointed and hurt and judgmental. She saw her husband as weak. She was ashamed that he was only a postal carrier. She couldn't see what the rest of us could. He was a sweet, kind man who loved her more than life itself. He was a good father and a good husband and a godly man. She saw only the things that weren't getting done around the house. In Romans it says, "Accept one another, then, just as Christ accepted you, in order to bring praise to God."[3]

Don't expect your husband to be something he cannot be. An introvert can never become an extrovert. A gentle man will never be the assertive person you want him to be. A forgetful husband may remain that way, no matter how much you nag and remind. A morning person will never feel comfortable staying up until all hours of the night. A big step toward your own happiness is learning to accept your husband as he is. He probably will always be that way. Trying to change a leopard's spots will never work. It will only make you unhappy.

Darlene's husband drove her nuts because of his forgetfulness. One day he ran to the grocery store to pick up hamburger buns for dinner, taking their young son with him. While there he was distracted by the pet store next door. He took his son in, and they looked at the fish for more than an hour. In the meantime, Darlene was home waiting for him to bring the buns for the now overcooked hamburgers. She thought he'd be right back. Things like this infuriated her. She saw them as directed at her.

Then she decided to accept her husband for who he was. She learned to relax and even laugh at his foibles. Recently, he forgot he'd taken the car to work and took the bus home. On his walk from the bus stop he passed a house where the people were moving out. He and Darlene were facing a move because the owner of their rental had sold their house. He asked the vacating family if their home was available for rental. They not only got the house, which was just a short distance from their own, but it was nicer than what they had and required only a small deposit to move in. They would never have known about the house if he'd driven the car home. Life can be difficult, but Darlene has decided to focus on the positive side of his forgetfulness.

Accept your own failings. Often in trying to be different from someone we end up being exactly like them. Learn to accept yourself for who you are. Learn to laugh at your own imperfections. I have this horrible need to do everything perfectly. I can't bear to make mistakes. What a relief when I finally admitted I wasn't perfect. In fact, I don't need to be perfect to be acceptable. Christ saved me while I was a sinner. Thank goodness he didn't wait until I was perfect. I'd still be on the outside looking in. Not only do I make mistakes, but I misspeak. I forget to do things that Larry has asked me to do. I miss appointments; I stumble over my words; housekeeping is not ever going to be my strength; I even say unkind things. I binge on food; I get sweaty; I even have underarm odor. I am human. Accepting that has made a world of difference in my happiness.

Learn to be satisfied with what you have. Paul tells us that this is the secret to happiness. "I have learned to be content whatever the circumstances. I know what it is to be in need, and I know what it is to have plenty. I have learned the secret of being content in any and every situation, whether well fed or hungry, whether living in plenty or in want."[4] I used to compare my home to the homes of my friends, and it never measured up. When someone would drop in, I would be ashamed of the stain on the carpet and the dirty dishes left on the counter. I would notice the cobwebs in the corner and streaks on my windows. During the entire visit I wondered what they thought, worrying that I didn't measure up.

Then I changed my thinking. God gave me everything I have, and my possessions are not what is most important. The person who has come to visit is. Now I focus on my visitor. I try to make them comfortable and draw out as much about them as I can. When they leave, instead of feeling miserable, I feel renewed at the wonderful sharing that took place.

I still live in the same house, I still am the same so-so housekeeper, but I don't notice the failings in my home and myself.

Put your expectations in the right place. There is only one source of happiness who will never let you down: Jesus Christ. When I turn to the world for my happiness, I'm disappointed. When I turn my hope to Jesus and my relationship with him, I'm never disappointed. I try not to expect anything. I write the first line of my life, and then I let Jesus fill in the next line. Every day I'm excited about what he'll reveal to me. I find joy in the azaleas blooming in my garden, a note from a friend, a smile from a child when I've helped him find the book in the library that he was looking for. My joy comes from inside me and is not dependent on anyone else's actions. My happiness doesn't rely on anything in this world, but only on what God wishes to give me. And I've never been disappointed. He has blessed me beyond what I could ever imagine.

❧

Action item: Make a list of the expectations you brought into your marriage. Pray over each one and ask God to remove your desire for each one.

CHAPTER NINE

I Don't Love Him

Love doesn't just sit there, like a stone, it has to be made,
like bread; re-made all the time, made new.
URSULA K. LEGUIN, *THE LATHE OF HEAVEN*, 1971[1]

*F*alling in love was the most wonderful thing that ever happened to me. Falling out of it the most painful. That rainy September day in 1969 when I said, "I do," I thought I loved this man who stood beside me. He opened doors and pulled out my chair. He knew what to order in restaurants and took me to see *Romeo and Juliet*. He put himself through college by pumping gas and changing oil in a service station and now had his first job in retailing. His future looked bright. I could talk about anything with him and he understood. He accepted me fully for who I was and wanted to spend the rest of his life with me. When we touched, electrical charges set off all sorts of wonderful feelings. I'd been told that the mad, crazy feelings we had for each other would fade, but that was okay because we were friends. When they were gone, we'd have that foundation to fall back on.

No one told me that someday I wouldn't even like him.

But it happened and I was devastated. The wonderful man whom I married disappeared and in his place was this cold, distant stranger who said terrible things to me and obviously no longer loved me. I felt lied to, cheated, guilty, and scared.

I think it was especially hard because I was a Christian. I believed that if I did all the right things, prayed, went to church, studied the Bible, and memorized scripture, then everything would go well for me. On Sunday morning, I was surrounded by people wearing their best clothes, their children behaving perfectly, smiles on their faces, and nothing but good things to say. The Bible study I attended was filled with couples who had nice homes, good jobs, and seemingly few struggles with their relationships. But I didn't feel that way, and when I looked at those happy people, I knew they wouldn't understand what I was going through. In fact, I feared they would condemn me because there must be something wrong with me spiritually.

I was scared and alone. I screamed at Larry because I wanted him to fix things. I wanted him to change back into the person he'd been so I could feel the love that had disappeared. The more I clung and cried, the more he withdrew. He couldn't understand what I was going through. I didn't understand what I was going through either. Everything I'd ever believed about love and marriage and living happily ever after was jerked out from under me.

In my years of working with married couples, I have come to believe that this "falling out of love" is a normal part of most marriages. Almost every couple comes to the point where one or both no longer feel "love" for the other partner.

No one tells us this is going to happen. If we are told, we refuse to believe it could happen to us. Instead our heads are full of romantic lies. Even in the church, we talk about how God has designed us for one person; it's our job to find him or her. When our marriages don't work out, we think it was because we were out of God's will when we married. I had one friend tell me that because she and her husband weren't Christians when they married, their marriage wasn't sanctioned by God. She left her husband for another man fully believing it was God's will.

This is not uncommon at all. In one month this last year I heard about three women from my church who left their husbands not because of adultery or abuse or addiction, but because they no longer loved them. I don't know these women personally, but not long ago I saw one of the husbands herding three little kids into church alone. My heart broke for all of them, the man who will suffer depression, the wife who one day will wake up and realize what she's done, and the kids who will probably never be all they could've been. They will grow up believing that Mommy no longer loves Daddy. Their lives will be filled with the fear that if Mommy can fall out of love with Daddy, then maybe she can fall out of love with them.

The world teaches that love is the glue that holds our marriages together, so when we "fall out of love" the marriage must be over. Is this true? Is this what Jesus modeled for us? Is this what the Bible teaches?

The answer is a resounding no. The Bible clearly teaches that love is only one of the three important ingredients of a happy, healthy relationship. The other two are respect and commitment. But before we discuss these, let's look at what the Bible has to say about love.

LOVE

There are basically three kinds of love. The first is romantic love. It's what we think of in our culture as being "in love." Usually there is hot, heavy breathing, and you can't sleep or eat or stop thinking about the person. Your emotions take wild swings from ecstasy to total despair. It's wonderful and it's awful at the same time. The idea of living without that person becomes unbearable. It's what we see on television and in the movies. It's romantic and wild and full of passion. I couldn't get enough of Larry's touch. We spent hours wrapped in each other's arms, holding hands, and, after we married, making love.

I think this kind of love is a blessing, but it's also a curse. In Genesis 3:16, God punished Eve and thus all womankind by saying that her desire would be for her husband. By all accounts this is not a positive thing. Most scholars believe that this "longing" is what causes unhappiness in women.[2] The Hebrew word for "desire" is *teshuwqah* (tesh-oo-kaw), and it means "longing or craving." It's used of a man for a woman and of a woman for a man, but also of an animal for devouring its prey. It is also used in Genesis 4:7: "Sin lies at the door. And its desire is for you" (NKJV). This desire, which brought us together, ultimately leads to our undoing because it's not permanent and cannot be filled by a person, but only by God.

Romantic love is a poor imitation of God's love. It is purely physical and can be incredibly powerful. It's the feeling that causes women to abandon their families to marry someone else, regardless of the consequences. I had a friend who left her husband for a man who had been married five times before. The craziness of it was so obvious to everyone, but she couldn't see it because she was being moved by romantic love.

This love can be addictive and can keep women trapped in violent or unhealthy relationships. I also believe it's what women are looking for when they marry over and over or get caught up in a series of affairs. It's an incredible high, but just like a drug high, there is the opposite low. This kind of feeling cannot be sustained and will disappear.

The second kind of love is what I call esteem. It refers to the feelings we have for our family and friends. This is a mutual fondness. We treat people who we believe are our friends kindly and affectionately. When I take my friend out to lunch for her birthday and when she sends me flowers to cheer me up, we are actively showing each other our friendship. It's a warm feeling of acceptance. It lasts as long as we believe the other esteems us and as long as it is mutual.

Thinking back I can count dozens of friends whom I loved. They were my best buddies from high school: Norma, Adelia, Judy, and Cheryl, who later became my roommate in college. Then there was Debbie who struggled through chemistry with me as we strove to become dietitians. All of them meant so much to me at the time. Now? I exchange Christmas cards with a few; the rest I've lost track of. It's not that I don't love them, but when the mutual experience stopped, so did the close friendship.

A marriage based on this kind of love alone probably won't last because we change. When Larry and I married, I would've told you we were very much alike, that we shared the same dreams and enjoyed the same things. But by year seven I couldn't see that we had anything much in common except two children. I thought I had fallen "out of love," and in a sense I had because these two kinds of love had passed away.

Now let me tell you about a third kind of love: *agape*. It's mature. It's not based on feelings and can be dispensed whether we get anything in return or not. God loves us in this way. He sent his Son to earth knowing that he would be rejected, spit upon, whipped, and finally executed. He didn't do it because we were deserving, but because he wanted to show his love for us—*even though we didn't return the affection*. It's the kind of love that is spoken of in our marriage vows when we say for richer, for poorer, in sickness, and in health. It's the kind of love that allows me to love my child even when he shouts in my face, "I hate you." It's the kind of love that gets me out of bed in the morning to make breakfast, clean toilets, or go to work every day.

In the King James Version of the Bible *agape* is translated as "charity." When we give a charitable contribution to a cause we care about, we do it expecting nothing in return. This is the kind of love that we are called to in 1 Corinthians 13. Even if this scripture is familiar to you, don't skip over it. Read it aloud.

> Though I speak with the tongues of men and of angels, but have not love, I have become sounding brass or a clanging cymbal. And though I have the gift of prophecy, and understand all mysteries and all knowledge, and though I have all faith, so that I could remove mountains, but have not love, I am nothing. And though I bestow all my goods to feed the poor, and though I give my body to be burned, but have not love, it profits me nothing. Love suffers long and is kind; love does not envy; love does not parade itself, is not puffed up; does not behave rudely, does not seek its own, is not provoked, thinks no evil; does not rejoice in iniquity, but rejoices in the truth; bears all things, believes all things, hopes all things, endures all things. Love never fails. But whether there are prophecies, they will fail; whether there are tongues, they will cease; whether there is knowledge, it will vanish away. For we know in part and we prophesy in part. But when that which is perfect has come, then that which is in part will be done away. When I was a child, I spoke as a child, I understood as a child, I thought as a child; but when I became a man, I put away childish things. For now we see in a mirror, dimly, but then face to face. Now I know in part, but then I shall know just as I also am known. And now abide faith, hope, love, these three; but the greatest of these is love.
>
> 1 CORINTHIANS 13:1–13, NKJV

Note two things about this passage. First, love is an action and second, it is our highest calling.

We are not called to "feel" love; we are called to "act" love. This was a revelation to me. I thought that I could do loving things only if I felt like doing them, but this scripture says nothing of the kind.

I can and in fact am commanded to do nice things for the people around me. I can take flowers to close relatives even though they show no affection for me. I can write a note telling my husband I love him and that I'm thinking about him, even though I don't feel like it. I can hold my tongue and not react to a hurtful comment from a patron at the library. I can be kind even when someone is not being kind to me. I can go on acting in a loving way even though I don't feel like it, and even though it's never returned to me.

This is what Jesus called me to do. It's what he called you to do.

I can tithe, teach Sunday school, sing in the choir, visit the poor, lead people to Christ, but all of these things are nothing in God's eyes if I don't love. And he wasn't just talking about our neighbor or the people we work with or our children. He was talking about our husbands. If we don't love them, then we are like a worthless noise, we are nothing; we are useless. Ouch!

When I first realized this, I was crushed. How could I possibly live with someone I didn't love? How could I do nice things for him? Wasn't I being hypocritical? No. I was only putting aside my childish idea of love, the romantic and the mutual esteem, and picking up the mature love of Christ. It's easy to love when we feel like it; even the most evil of men can do that. The mark of a Christian is to love even when we don't feel like it and even though we never receive anything in return. "If you love those who love you, what reward will you get? Are not even the tax collectors doing that? And if you greet only your brothers, what are you doing more than others? Do not even pagans do that?" (Matthew 5:46–47).

Christ loves every man and every woman and every child on this earth, not just those who accept him and not just those who love him in return. He was beaten until he was unrecognizable. He was spat upon and mocked and scorned. Large spikes were driven into his ankles and through his wrists, and he hung on that cross in unthinkable pain for each one of us.

When I compared my suffering to that, I began to feel puny.

When this truth finally got through to my heart, I turned to a new way of living. I acted loving even though I didn't feel like it and even though I didn't feel it returned. At times I blew it completely and wanted to give up. I had days when I cried bitter tears because it seemed so unfair to be giving and giving and seemingly getting nothing in return. But I clung to the scripture promise that if I did it God's way, I would find "a whole, healed, put-together life right now, with more and more of life on the way! . . . God's gift is *real life*, eternal life, delivered by Jesus, our Master."[3]

And when I was weak Jesus was right alongside helping me. He gave me the power I needed to hold my tongue. He gave me the courage I needed to ask Larry for his forgiveness for being critical or quarrelsome or selfish. He filled my life with wonderful friends and opportunities to minister to other women.

The real rewards came at unexpected times like when I would look out the window and see my children playing baseball in the backyard with their dad. Or when we all piled into the car and went to church together as a family. Or when a junior-high teacher said, "Your son is a great kid. I hope you have more Bodmers coming my way."

RESPECT

Love is only one leg of a three-legged stool.

When I was growing up, my dad had milk cows and I used to watch him milk. He used a stool that had one leg. He'd sidle up to that cow and sit down on that stool and within a few minutes have that cow milked. It looked easy. But when I tried sitting on that stool, I fell over. A one-legged stool is precarious at best. To be truly strong you need three legs. Love is only one leg; the other two legs are respect and commitment.

When Larry and I married I was nineteen and he was twenty-three. He had a quick sense of humor and knew a lot about business, fixing cars, investing money, music, art, photography, and politics. Our conversations covered a myriad of topics, and he was more knowledgeable than I on most of them. I trusted his opinion on just about everything except grocery shopping, cooking, and child rearing. He knew exactly what he wanted out of life and how to get it.

Over the next few years something astonishing happened to this funny, smart, decisive person I married. He suddenly couldn't make a decision, and when he did they were often wrong. He became dull-witted and humorless and boring. He said the most astonishing things to friends and could never get the facts straight when telling a story. I pointed out to him how he could improve himself or a better way he could do things, but he refused to change.

He became surly and defensive, spending more and more time at work, out in the yard, or glued to the television set. We went from close friends to strangers living in the same house. We never had much to say to each other, and when we did talk we usually argued.

The problem wasn't only that I'd fallen out of love, but that I'd fallen out of respect too.

How important is this to a marriage? Nowhere in the Bible are wives commanded to love their husbands. But in Ephesians there is a clear command that we respect them. "However, each one of you also must love his wife as he loves himself, and the wife must respect her husband" (Ephesians 5:33).

Why? Because God knows this is the hardest thing for us to do, and he knows it's what our husbands desire most from us. According to the commentaries that I've read, it has a lot to do with what happened in the Garden of Eden. Before the Fall women were equal to men, but afterward God told Eve and thus all of womankind, "Your desire shall be for your husband, and he shall rule over you" (Genesis 3:16, NKJV). The word *rule* is translated from *mashal* (maw-shal) and means "dominion, to reign, rule, or have power."[4] Women went from equality to being ruled over—the very last thing any of us want.

We constantly struggle against this headship. If you doubt me, look at the modern women's-rights movement or just listen to women discussing the passage in Ephesians 5 where it says women shall be in submission to their husbands. We don't like to be ruled over. One way to get out from under any authority is to disrespect it. Look at what teenagers do to their parents, students to their teachers, or workers to their bosses.

One woman told me that her first husband went from being a strong, decisive person to a weakling who looked to her for all the answers. Another told me it was as if he became afraid of her, and backed down from every argument, leaving her feeling disgusted with him and confused about her role. Many women struggle against negative, disrespectful thoughts about their husbands.

Join this with the physical desire we discussed earlier, and you can see that it can become not just a physical desire, but a positional one. One commentator said, "Her sexual attraction for the man, and his headship over her (will become sources of) trouble and anguish rather than unalloyed joy and blessing."[5] We want not only to be equal but to be in charge. If you think this isn't true, then just examine your own marriage. Do you think your husband makes better decisions than you do? Do you think he's smarter? Do you think the way he does things is the right way, or could you do it better? Most of us think we are superior to our spouses in almost every aspect of life. We're better drivers, better parents, better at giving directions, better at yard work, and better at handling money. We might relinquish car repairs to our husbands, but that's because machines often seem a mystery to us.

Loving my husband at all times was simple compared to struggling to be willingly submissive to his leadership.

Get control of your thought life.
What do you think about? I often find myself making mental judgments. I don't like the way my husband eats his cereal, prunes our

trees and shrubs, cuts the grass, takes care of the checkbook, pays the bills, spends money, drives the car, falls asleep in front of the TV, grinds his teeth—well, you get the idea.

One way to stop these negative thoughts is to nip them in the bud. Whenever a critical thought comes into your head, instead of dwelling on it, turn it into something positive. I might mow the grass differently, but at least I don't have to do it. I might balance the checkbook to the penny, but his way does save time. I don't fall asleep in front of the TV, but then Larry fixes my breakfast, allowing me to sleep longer so I get more rest. Philippians says, "Finally, brethren, whatever things are true, whatever things are noble, whatever things are just, whatever things are pure, whatever things are lovely, whatever things are of good report, if there is any virtue and if there is anything praiseworthy—meditate on these things."[6]

Satan would love to control your thought life. When he does, he can destroy your marriage, your self-esteem, your faith, and your happiness. Even if you never say any of these negative thoughts aloud, they creep into your nonverbal conversation. The way you look at your husband, the way you listen to what he says, how you interrupt him when he's speaking, or how you interfere when he's disciplining your children. These actions shout to him your lack of respect. From there it's a downward spiral. As he struggles to regain your respect, he makes more and more mistakes, increasing your disdain, therefore worsening his own self-doubt. He may act like a total wimp or a big bully trying to win your respect. Not liking the person he is when he's around you, he withdraws more and more, pretending he doesn't care what you think. He becomes exactly what you thought he was. Rein in your negative thoughts and this battle can be won. "Take captive every thought to make it obedient to Christ."[7]

Apply the principles from chapter 6. Admit it to God when you catch yourself thinking negatively. Continually humble yourself and ask for God's forgiveness. Ask him to change you from the inside out. Ask him to give you new eyes so you can see your husband clearly.

Recognize your differences.

Often what I was being critical of was in fact just a difference. One of the things that drove me crazy was the way Larry answers questions. Just this morning I asked him something about this chapter. Before he answered I ate my toast, planned my grocery list, and organized my day. It seemed to take him an eternity to answer. I used to think this was because he wasn't very clever. What I've come to appreciate is that Larry carefully considers every word that comes out of his mouth. I on the other hand think as I talk, which gets me into a whole lot of trouble. I've often said that the only time I open my mouth is to change feet. Larry's slow answer does not mean he's a slow thinker. In fact, he's incredibly wise and highly esteemed by his fellow pastors, coworkers, and friends. They often seek him out for advice because he's a gifted counselor. He doesn't give them off-the-top-of-his-head advice, but deep insights that help.

I like deep, psychological movies; he wants lots of action. He's a morning person; I'm a night owl. I like coffee; he likes tea. One is not better than the other; they are just different. We don't have to agree on everything. Recognizing this can lead to much understanding and peace.

Instead of dwelling on the differences, learn to think about how much you're alike. We both like warm baths, walks in parks, antique shopping, and popcorn with our movies. We share a mutual love of Jesus Christ and enjoy our people-oriented ministries. We have similar political and theological views. We both think our two sons are about the most excellent people to ever walk the face of this earth and are awed at their bright minds and many gifts.

Differences make you more complete as a couple. I was the strict disciplinarian; Larry softened my harshness. I'm more outgoing, which draws Larry into social settings. Larry's deep faith has led him into the ministry, which has caused me to stretch into areas that make me uncomfortable but are good for me. We each would be less if we were not a couple. Learning to appreciate this has helped my respect grow.

Finally, learn to laugh. There's nothing like a good-humored chuckle over your differences to make them not seem so awful. We laugh over the way Larry picks out a parking space now, but before it was a real sore spot. We laugh at my backseat driving, which before led to many arguments and hard feelings.

Place your husband back in authority.

Recently we were having dinner with some friends. The husband launched into a wonderful story about their vacation. The wife kept interrupting, setting the details straight. "No it wasn't chicken we had, it was salmon." "It was Margaret, dear, not Susan." "We were there until nine and it was cold." I know my friend just thought she was being the color commentator, setting the facts straight, telling the story as she remembered. But her constant corrections were disrespectful. And I'm as guilty as anyone. What difference does it make to the listener who said what, when we don't even know the people? And what if she's wrong? Memory is a funny thing; recent studies show that two people who witness the same event will remember totally different things. She's interrupting him for no reason. A wise woman will recognize this and keep quiet. Let her husband have the glory of the attention of the group as he shares his story.

Another thing we can do to help our husbands feel respected is to ask them for advice. "Honey, I'm having this problem with a coworker. Can you help me?" Men are fixers. The highest compliment one man can give another is to ask for advice.

The next highest compliment you can give him is to listen. When he finishes a sentence, pause a minute before you reply. Don't read the paper, watch the TV, or yell at the kids. Give him your full attention, eye to eye. You probably did that when you were dating. Now would be a good time to start that again.

Tell him when he does something right.
Encouragement is such a simple thing, but it can make a tremendous difference to your husband. Tell him when he does something right. Thank him for fixing the faucet or finding someone who will. Tell him when he makes a good decision or says something wise or clever. Compliment him when he dresses well. Point out the positives in his life.

When he helps you with the dishes, don't, I repeat DO NOT tell him that he loaded the dishwasher wrong or forgot to scrub the egg off the forks. Don't remake the bed after he's through or point out the streaks he left on the windows he just washed.

Continually ask yourself, Is this issue more important than our relationship?

Let him make mistakes.
Recently we went car shopping. Before we even started I resolved to let Larry pick out the one he wanted. Why? Because the last two were purchases that I made. Oh yes, Larry was there making the decision with me, but I coerced him into buying the cars I wanted, and neither one of them turned out to be a good decision. This time I determined to let Larry pick, even if it was a mistake. We looked at several makes and models of used cars and drove a couple of them around the block. I fought to keep my mouth shut and only said something when asked. I did urge him to get the one he wanted, not the one that was the cheapest. The result? He bought a slightly used fairly priced car with all the bells and whistles that men love. When his friends admire it, I see him swell with pride and I feel a deep sense of satisfaction.

But I learned this the hard way. Another decision that I made against Larry's will is lying on the carpet beside me. She's blind in one eye, totally deaf, and can hardly walk due to the arthritis in her spine. She's cost us thousands of dollars in vet bills, once completely wiping out our savings account. Flea control has become a major focus of my life. Larry fought me good and hard on this one, but I fought back and I fought dirty. I got our children involved. Not only did he have to refuse me, but he also had to refuse two boys with big eyes and longing hearts. Now there are many days I wish I'd listened to him.

But what if your husband makes the wrong decision? Letting our husbands fail is difficult. One woman told me that she and her husband had just bought a brand-new house and they were having battles over the correct way to plant a yard. She said, "I can't let him do it his way. It will be all wrong, and I'll have to live with the consequences."

I asked her what was most important: a yard that drains well or her relationship with her husband? A few problems with grass or her husband's self-worth? Besides, he'll have to live with the consequences, too, not just her.

My husband has made plenty of wrong decisions. Accepting an ill-advised job offer resulted in his being out of work for almost a year. We had a mortgage, a new baby, and bills to pay, but we made it through. We never went hungry, and we never got behind in our bills. Looking back I can see that my attitude would have made all the difference during this time. Instead of trusting God's provision, I panicked. Fear was my constant companion, and I struck out in anger. It's no wonder that Larry withdrew into the sanctity of his garage. Honestly, I was not a nice person. How different things would have been if I had trusted what God and Larry were doing. I just pray you can learn from my mistake.

Let me tell you about the hardest decision I ever made. We have two boys. They were only a year apart in school. This meant that within one year they'd both be gone after graduating from high school. I saw that coming when they were about four and five years old. My heart yearned for another baby—a girl. Someone I could teach to sew and knit, someone whom I could share my femininity with. After years of living in a house full of men, I longed to see frills and lace and hair ribbons.

However, Larry didn't want another baby. He felt the financial pressure of another mouth to feed. I argued about how much love another child would bring and that God would provide, but I could tell that this would be just too much pressure. There were days I was tempted to accidentally forget my birth control. There were times I cried out to God to change Larry's mind. God reminded me of Sarah and Abraham who went out of God's will, resulting in Ishmael's birth. Taking matters into their own hands, they answered their own prayer in a way that has caused nothing but strife for Arabs and Jews down through the ages. Learning from this disastrous example, I determined to let it be God's way. I waited for Larry's decision.

As my thirties slowly slipped away, I felt the fear of this never being resolved. I looked at every little girl baby and longed for her to be mine. My sister's two daughters, so full of love for their aunt Judy, made me ache for my own sweet girl.

But I trusted and I waited and I prayed. The day I turned forty was the hardest day of my life. I have no daughter to hold and will never have one. It has been hard to forgive Larry for not giving this precious gift to me. He jokes that we probably would've had another boy. There is no happy ending to this story. There's only a deep sense of peace that I did the right thing and that God will reward me for not undermining my husband's authority. Perhaps it will be two wonderful daughters-in-law who will be closer to me than my own would've been. Perhaps it will be granddaughters that will fill my ache. Until then I will trust and love and forgive.

A funny thing happens when we start this process of respect. Our husbands begin to feel better about themselves, so we see more traits to respect, which leads them to grow in confidence and ability, which leads to more respect. It can begin with you. It's your decision. I love the way *The Living Bible* translates the verse in Ephesians: "The wife must see to it that she deeply respects her husband—obeying, praising and honoring him" (Ephesians 5:33, TLB).

COMMITMENT

The last component of a successful marriage is commitment. The day I exchanged my wedding vows with Larry, we gained a partner. We may not have recognized him at the time, but God became a part of our commitment to each other. We vowed before him to love, honor, and obey until death separated us. Not until we fell out of love, not until we fell out of respect, but until death. And God is right alongside us, helping us, urging us on, cheering for our victories.

Your vows may have been words, lightly spoken, but don't take them lightly. Divorce was never a part of God's plan. He only allowed it because of our hard hearts.

Marriages and families are falling apart. "The Census Bureau estimates that more than six out of every ten children born in the mid-nineties will live in a single-parent home before they reach their eighteenth birthday."[8] The result is a whole generation of children who are growing up without the stable influence of a father and a mother. Why not stop that dire prediction right now, beginning with your family, your marriage?

I don't tell you to stay married because I want you to live a miserable life. I tell you to stick it out because I think the reward for staying and working far outweighs the sacrifices you will need to make.

❧

Action item: Ask your husband to make a list of ten things you can do for him that he would interpret as your expression of love for him. Do one of them every week for the next ten weeks when he least expects it.

CHAPTER TEN

We Can't Talk

> *I do not understand what I do. For what I want to do I do not do,*
> *but what I hate I do.*
>
> ROMANS 7:15

I can spend hours talking to close friends sharing my innermost fears, loves, and weaknesses and come away feeling enlivened and affirmed. For years I tried to re-create this level of communication with my husband, and was left with frustration and confusion.

He couldn't seem to hear what I had to say. Almost every effort to engage him in conversation ended in one or the other of us being angry or hurt. Since I obviously had no trouble talking to my friends, I came to the conclusion that the problem had to be his. There was something wrong with him. Perhaps he'd been dropped as a child or emotionally damaged when he went through the horror of junior high or traumatized when he became a father.

Experts tell us that men only have so many words to say, and by the time they get home at night they've used up their quota. That's no comfort when you're hungry to tell him about your day, your frustrations with the children or your job, your worries that there won't be enough money to put the children through college or to retire or buy a home. The price of milk and gas just went up again, and your income just won't cover the cost of little Jimmy's braces. Even good news like your children's good grades or the good deal you found at a garage sale can be put on the back burner. Knowing that your husband has used up his quota of words for the day won't take away your loneliness or allay the fear that he doesn't love you anymore.

One answer is to just accept that this is the way he is and go on with your life. But this attitude can lead to a less than fulfilling marriage for both of you. I think there's a better answer, and it begins with refusing to believe the experts.

My husband is a counselor. He spends all day listening to people and sharing comforting words of wisdom with them. He's actually gifted in this area. That means he's a gifted communicator. Let me repeat: He's a gifted communicator. I'm willing to bet your husband is a good communicator, too, or at least has better verbal skills than you think. Look at what he does for a living. Unless he's in a very unique business setting, his communication skills are what make him good at his job.

So if my husband is capable and perhaps even skilled in this area, then there must be other reasons why he's not talking or listening to me.

Reason One: An Untamed Tongue

I tend to talk off the top of my head. I say what comes into my mind the moment it arrives. It's my way of thinking; I've just learned this about myself recently. I can mull things over and over in my head, but until I actually hear myself speak aloud, I often don't know what I believe about something. I need someone to bounce my thoughts off of before I can come to a decision. That can be scary for my husband. For example, when I say aloud I want to remodel the kitchen, he hears: MAJOR RENOVATION. Alarm bells start going off in his head about the cost and the amount of time it will take. He begins to formulate all the reasons why we can't do it. He squashes my idea, not because he doesn't love me, but because my thinking aloud my half-formed thought scares him. He doesn't understand that I just want to dream a little, plan for the future, find out just how complicated the job will be, and discuss what we can afford.

Another example is when I say, "I feel lonely." My desire is to tell him how I am feeling so we can talk about it and perhaps come to some resolutions on how to spend more time together. Unfortunately, he hears: You are a bad husband; you are not doing your job or I wouldn't be feeling this way. Instead of giving me the sympathy that I'm looking for, he reacts defensively. This may seem unreasonable, but many men are wired this way. That's why bad feelings can arise over something that seems very simple. This is particularly true during times of stress.

During our bad years, as the distance between us grew, I would say hateful things like: "You don't love me anymore." "You don't care about me." "You never think about me." "I wish I'd never married you." I said these things not because I hated Larry, but because I was hurting and I wanted him to see through my words and into my heart. In James there is this incredible scripture that's like an arrow piercing my heart every time I read it. "All kinds of animals, birds, reptiles and creatures of the sea are being tamed and have been tamed by man, but no man can tame the tongue. It is a restless evil, full of deadly poison. With the tongue we praise our Lord and Father, and with it we curse men, who have been made in God's likeness. Out of the same mouth come praise and cursing. My brothers, this should not be."[1]

Getting control of my tongue was and still is a daily, hourly, minute-by-minute challenge. But it was a must if I was going to improve the communication between us. If you're struggling with communication, the following suggestions will help:

Run your half-formed thoughts by someone else first. If you don't have a close friend, find one. Women need someone to talk to, but don't turn these conversations into a husband bashing. Use this time in a positive way to discover how you think and feel about certain issues. Pick your friend carefully. You don't want someone who will fill you with negative thoughts. A strong, older Christian woman would be ideal. Take her to lunch.

Begin your sentences with disclaimers. They go something like this, "Honey I've been thinking a little about the future, and I want to run some things by you to see what you think." "What I have to say may be hard to listen to, but I need to talk to you about it. Will you try to listen?" These disclaimers prepare him and allay his fears before they even can surface.

Spend time talking to God. A daily time with God is a must. Run all the garbage that's in your heart and mind by him. He hears everything and loves you anyway. Let him heal your hurts before you take them to your husband. Ask for his wisdom in dealing with an issue.

Ask forgiveness when you fail. You will fail, I promise. The good news is that part of a relationship is asking forgiveness and learning to accept it.

Learn to say negative things in a positive way. Ephesians 4:29 says, "Don't use foul or abusive language. Let everything you say be good and helpful, so that your words will be an encouragement to those who hear them" (NLT). One of our issues was Larry getting home from work on time. With two babies crying at my knees and dinner either burning or becoming very overcooked, my nerves were frazzled by the time he walked through the door. I would strike out and say something like this: "You are thoughtless. Why didn't you call? How can you do this to me?"

A better way to handle this is to put myself aside for a moment and concentrate on him, not as someone who is powerless, but as someone who is making the decision to do something loving. I could say, "I'm happy you're home. Was the traffic bad?" That would give him an opening to let me know why he was late. After listening to him and sympathizing, then and only then will I have earned the right to say, "I was worried. I thought maybe you'd been in an accident." Later, I could tell him how the kids were driving me crazy and how much I hated for dinner to be ruined and ask if he could please call me the next time. The chances of his hearing me, and actually changing his ways, increase about 50 percent when he doesn't feel attacked.

Learning to turn a negative into a positive can be challenging, but with practice you can do it. Proverbs 25:15 says, "Through patience a ruler can be persuaded, and a gentle tongue can break a bone."

Don't share everything. I thought one of the most important parts of marriage was the need to be totally honest. On the surface this sounds good, but in reality it can be damaging. I don't think you need to share every little thing that comes into your head. For one reason, what may be true today, may not be true tomorrow—especially when it comes to your emotions. They can range from one extreme to another based on your monthly hormone fluctuations, lack of sleep, the weather, or a myriad of other physical reasons.

Before I share anything that may hurt my husband, I ask myself, "Will it make our relationship better in the long run?" If the answer is no, then I keep it to myself. If the answer is yes, even though it is painful, I share it, but only after much prayer. By doing this, I've been able to finally get through to Larry about some of the areas in our lives that have needed changing. After a long talk about how overwhelmed I was by the housework, we came up with a simple solution. Whoever cooks dinner doesn't have to do dishes. How wonderful to sit in the living room after dinner and watch the news, while Larry takes care of the pots and pans. By bringing only the important issues to him, he's more willing to listen to me, whereas before he felt overwhelmed by my complaints and didn't always know which ones to address and which ones to ignore.

Some husbands can't take any criticism. James 5:16 says, "The effective, fervent prayer of a righteous man avails much" (NKJV). The word *avail* means "powerful, able to force something to happen." If you are right in your relationship with God, then he will hear your prayers and do something with this man you're trying to live with. In some churches prayer has been reduced to a cliché. I've come to believe it's a powerful tool that should never be underestimated.

With your tongue you can bless your husband or curse him. If you want to renew your relationship, you will need to learn to control this "deadly" weapon.

REASON TWO: AN UNWILLINGNESS TO BE DIRECT

I used to believe that part of the reason Larry didn't hear me was because I didn't explain myself properly; so I would reword my statements and try again. I went on and on and on in hopes that the third or fourth explanation would get through to him. What I've since learned is that my verbiage was actually a turnoff. The more I said, the less he listened. I've learned to say what I have to say and then hush.

Don't use your words to manipulate. "And don't say anything you don't mean. . . . Just say 'yes' and 'no.' When you manipulate words to get your own way, you go wrong."² For years I hinted at what I wanted from Larry. I thought coming right out and asking was wrong. I don't know how many times I ended up hurt because Larry didn't get the hint that I wanted to be taken out to dinner.

"I'm tired, honey; I had a hard day. I forgot to take the meat out of the freezer; now what am I going to fix?" I said.

"Can't you thaw it out in the microwave?" he asked. In his mind he was being helpful; in my mind he was being cruel because I wanted him to take me out to dinner. I have this romantic notion that he should be able to read my mind. I remember once going shopping with him and looking at spatulas.

"Oh, look," I said, "here's one of those spatulas I've been wanting." After looking at the price I added, "But it's so expensive." I wanted him to say, "Go ahead and buy it. You're worth it." Instead he just wandered on. I was hurt and angry because he was so thoughtless. I pouted for a few more aisles and then decided I had to say something. He was totally amazed. Then I realized I hadn't asked him to buy it for me, I'd only hinted. He was more than glad to buy me what I wanted. I would've saved him and myself some agony if only I'd been direct. Jeremiah 9:8 says, "[The] tongue is a deadly arrow; it speaks with deceit. With [her] mouth each speaks cordially to [her] neighbor, but in her heart [she] sets a trap for him."

REASON THREE: OUR WORDS DON'T MATCH OUR ACTIONS

One of the things that I used to throw back in Larry's face when he accused me of saying something was, "I never said that." I would be indignant and defend my position to the death. But the following statistic made me aware of something I was doing that was far more damaging than my actual words. A study done by Albert Mehrabian of Yale University showed that our words are the most insignificant part of communication.[3]

Words alone—7 percent
Body language—55 percent
Tone of voice—38 percent

You see, in my self-righteous attitude I could say that I never "said" the wrong thing. Just like the Sadducees and Pharisees of

Jesus' time, I was clean on the outside, but on the inside I was full of anger and hate. I let it show through the other two parts of communication: body language and tone of voice. The look in my eyes, my angry tone, the way I crossed my arms, all shouted loud and clear what was in my heart. I thought if Larry couldn't read my mind then he wouldn't know how I felt about something. But he knew, and he had every right to call me on my judgmental attitude.

Learning to be honest from the inside out has been hard. I've spent much time on my face before God asking his forgiveness, working on my attitude, and searching to find the right words to say. You can get control. Just continue to practice forgiveness on a moment-to-moment basis. Work on your own faults, let the Holy Spirit work in you, grow closer to God, and as you do, he will change you on the inside. Then your words will begin to match your tone of voice and body language and vice versa.

And when you are faithful, the Holy Spirit will begin to work on your husband in ways you never thought possible. He will change and become the man you want, not in your time and not through your manipulation, but in God's time and through his love.

REASON FOUR: SELF-DEFENSIVENESS

We have a black and white cat named Puffin. Next door to us lives a white cat named Mike. Not a day goes by that we don't find the pair of them locked in some kind of battle. It usually consists of their staring and hissing at each other with the hairs on their backs at full attention. Finally, one of them will slink away in defeat, only to return the next day for another round. That's a picture of how Larry and I lived. We had hurt each other so often and in so many areas of our lives that we could hardly talk without raising each other's hackles. The issues ranged from money to religion, discipline of our children, help around the house, absence of affection, backseat driving, lack of respect, and on and on. Healing our scars so that we could live together in peace seemed like an impossible task—even for God.

One of the things that helped was learning to make "I" statements instead of "you" statements. Some examples of "you" statements are:

> You make me angry.
> You never help around the house.
> You're always late.
> You are thoughtless.

These are judgmental in nature and immediately raise my husband's defenses. When his defenses are up, all communication stops. Particularly damaging are the words *always* and *never*. Whenever I use those two words, his immediate response is to name the times when he did help around the house and when he was on time. Changing these comments to "I" statements may seem rather trivial, but the difference it makes is surprising.

You make me angry.	I'm feeling angry.
You never help around the house.	Will you empty the dishwasher?
You're always late.	I was worried because you were late.
You are thoughtless.	I'm feeling like no one wants to play with me.

Can you see the difference? Instead of judgments, I'm trying to communicate my feelings. These don't always imply that Larry is doing something wrong; it's amazing how much better he listens to me.

It's natural to react defensively to criticism, but for the sake of your marriage it's good to learn to control that reaction. You can do this by taking a deep breath, thinking through carefully what is being said, and choosing not to say anything in your own defense. This will take practice, but it is possible.

One thing that has helped me is to accept the fact that although I am a sinner, just like everyone else, God loves me anyway. This has done more to advance my self-esteem than any accomplishment or compliment ever did. Jesus called us to take on the following attitude:

> If you have any encouragement from being united with Christ, if any comfort from his love, if any fellowship with the Spirit, if any tenderness and compassion, then make my joy complete by being like-minded, having the same love, being one in spirit and purpose. Do nothing out of selfish ambition or vain conceit, but in humility consider others better than yourselves. Each of you should look not only to your own interests, but also to the interests of others.
>
> Your attitude should be the same as that of Christ Jesus.
>
> PHILIPPIANS 2:1–5

Jesus accepted criticism. You can too. Look at it as an opportunity to grow. And if it's not valid, then reject it. But don't defend and don't react angrily.

REASON FIVE: WE DON'T LISTEN

Listening is the key to getting your husband to open up and communicate with you even about his most intimate fears. If he's tried in the past and become frustrated, he may slowly stop talking about all sorts of areas in his life. Familiarity breeds bad habits. Here are a few:

Criticizing. Holding your tongue is critical to keeping the channels of communication open. Contrary to what men would have us believe, they have fragile egos. They need our approval and acceptance as much as we need theirs.

Giving unwanted advice. Larry often wants me to be a sounding board. He just needs me to listen as he talks over his problem. If I jump in too quickly with a solution, then he will correctly judge that I'm not listening or that I don't care.

Letting your motor run. That means don't let your mind wander or make assumptions or assume you know what he's going to say while your husband is talking. Concentrate on him and forget the myriad of other things that are going on in your life. Turn the TV off, turn the radio off. Get rid of all distractions and hear what he's saying.

Answering for him. It takes Larry a minute or two to answer a question. I have to give him that time, or he becomes frustrated. It's a real struggle not to jump in with more of my thoughts and ideas or finish his sentences for him. When you've been married a long time, you just assume you know what your spouse is going to say, but you may be wrong. In fact you might have learned something new about your husband, something he never told you before, but you cut him short by filling in the blanks.

Interrupting. I have someone in my life who never lets me finish my sentences. Before I'm done speaking, she begins talking. I know she never heard what I was saying. This drives me nuts, and I find I avoid being with her.

Are you guilty of doing this? When I pay attention to my speaking habits, I realize I often am guilty of this same behavior. I do it because I assume I know what the speaker is going to say before they've even finished speaking.

Jumping in too quickly. I read once that it's a sign of respect to pause for a moment before replying to someone. What an easy way to show respect to our husbands.

Listening is a fine art, which developed can lead to better communication, even if only one of you practices it. In James it says, "Let every man be swift to hear."[4] Much unhappiness would be avoided if we practiced this simple rule.

REASON SIX: WE DON'T GIVE OUR HUSBANDS ENOUGH SPACE

Too much closeness can lead to smothering. Let your husband have a place where he can go to be alone, such as the garage or basement or garden or a favorite chair in front of the TV. A good friend of mine said that when she needed to talk to her husband about something, and it didn't seem that he was listening, she would follow him around the house and even out to his workshop explaining her thought process. No matter how carefully she worded her thoughts, often these encounters ended with his getting angry. After years of frustration, she finally learned to say what she wanted in simple, straightforward terms and then gave her husband space to think about it. It might take him a few hours or even days, but he would come back to her, after having thought it through completely, and they would resolve the issue.

Many husbands are like this. If we are going on and on, they can't think. They begin to feel manipulated and controlled by our words. This behavior can drive your husband crazy. Learn to state what you want and then be still and give him space.

REASON SEVEN: OUR WORDS GET IN THE WAY

One of the tools we learned to use on our Marriage Encounter weekend was a letter. When oversensitivity to tone of voice and body language is a problem, then the written word can be a real blessing. A spoken word is out there for both of you to hear, but a written word can be erased. It can be a helpful tool, especially during this time of struggle.

A word of caution. I know a woman who was too afraid to tell her husband how unhappy she was, so she wrote him a letter. He never responded to it, and she's too apprehensive to ask why. Of course she's terribly hurt by this because she believes he doesn't care. My advice to her would have been to be there when he read it. Don't write a letter releasing a bombshell without being there to discuss it. Men don't know how to handle these things. They don't know how to bring them up. They often just want to ignore problems and hope they'll go away. Another solution would have been to make a date to discuss the contents. A letter is a tool, but it won't replace good solid communication skills.

❧

Action item: Take your weakest communication point (listening, interrupting, letting your motor run, etc.) and work on improving it this week.

CHAPTER ELEVEN

I Feel So Angry

*Peace I leave with you, My peace I give to you; not as the world
gives do I give to you. Let not your heart be troubled,
neither let it be afraid.*
JOHN 14:27, NKJV

I work at a local library. On Friday nights we sponsor a program
that may draw one hundred extra people. For three hours we have
crying babies, students who need help finding articles on AIDS,
upset patrons with fines on their cards who are positive they
returned their books on time, and a program to get ready. This last
week after things settled down, a fellow worker asked, "How do you
stay so calm in all this chaos?"

Cool, calm, and *collected* are adjectives that have been used to
describe me over the years. People don't know that my cool, calm
exterior has come at a high price. Underneath, I'm a boiling mass of
emotions. I've just learned to hide them. I suspect it started when I
was little. My aunts, sister, and cousins have reported to me that I
threw temper tantrums as a child. Not only would I throw myself on

the floor kicking and screaming, I'd hold my breath until I passed out. They used words like *spoiled, frightening,* and *shameful.* In the telling, I got the message—anger is wrong, anger is bad. And so I, a mass of emotions, began a lifetime of learning to hide those feelings. This worked pretty well with casual acquaintances and even good friends. But under the intense intimacy of marriage, my resolve to never be angry broke down. What I experienced I call the Anger Cycle. Here is how it works:

THE ANGER CYCLE

Phase One: I resolve never to be angry, especially over those little things like when Larry plays solitaire while he talks to me on the phone, falls asleep in the middle of movies that I like, or crunches his cereal with his spoon before he takes the first bite. I'm better than that. I'm mature; we are mature. We can talk things through with calm resolve. These issues are petty. The marks of a good Christian are patience and self-control.[1] To be anything less than that is to fail.

Besides, people don't like women who yell and scream. I want to be liked. Anger is unacceptable; I just won't let myself feel it, then I'll never have to show it.

Phase Two: When I do feel anger, I ignore it. Larry forgets to record a check in the check register. He promises to get my car fixed but never finds time to call the repair shop. When I come home late at night, the garage door is closed. He forgot to leave it open for me, and I have to climb out of my car in the rain to open it. I fight the mean things that are going on in my head. *He's thoughtless. He obviously doesn't care about me. He could have been more careful.* But I don't say anything. I don't want to start a fight. I want to be nice.

Phase Three: Something happens that pushes me over the edge. Larry comes home from work. He yells at the boys for leaving their bicycles in the driveway and wants to know why the lawn hasn't been mowed. I try to explain that the boys had extra baseball practice, but he's not listening. Later, he complains about his job and I don't want to hear it. I'm tired too. I say, "Why don't you look for another one instead of complaining all the time?" He says, "You don't care about me." I say, "I do too." He says something about his shirts not being ironed.

Phase Four: I blow up. He sits there as if he's done nothing wrong. I remind him of the five other things he's done that were thoughtless. He defends himself. I scream; he shouts. I say horrible things; he says them back. I'm angry with him and myself because I'm blowing it one more time. I hate the way I'm acting, but I don't know how to stop. We both go to bed angry, nothing solved.

Phase One: I resolve never to get angry. . . .

For years I lived on this merry-go-round, searching for peace but finding only unrest. With each revolution it became harder and harder to control my anger. The fights increased in intensity and duration. They went from once in nine months, to monthly, then weekly, then to feeling angry all the time. The only way of escape from this interminable ride seemed to be divorce. Unfortunately I would have taken the same thinking with me into my next relationship. The real solution was to stop this devastating cycle.

It wasn't until I started dealing with my anger in a healthy way that I found peace. Now my cool, calm, and collected exterior has become how I truly feel on the inside. If this sounds familiar, here are the twelve steps that helped me end this unhealthy cycle.

1. Acknowledge your anger.

I get angry. It's part of my human nature. To deny this feeling is to deny myself. But isn't that what we're trying to do? Aren't we trying to deny, even for the best of reasons, that we are human? In the Old Testament God expressed his anger many times with those stubborn Jews. Many of the most highly thought of men in the

Bible got angry: Moses with the pharaoh,[2] Paul with Ananias,[3] and Jesus with the Sadducees and Pharisees.[4] Then of course there is the famous scene at the temple where Jesus completely blew up. "He made a whip out of cords, and drove all from the temple area, both sheep and cattle; he scattered the coins of the money changers and overturned their tables. To those who sold doves he said, 'Get these out of here! How dare you turn my Father's house into a market!'"(John 2:15–16).

Jesus raged about like a bull, throwing over tables and whipping the money changers. If anger is so awful, then Jesus would never have expressed it that way. Let's look at what Scripture says about this misunderstood feeling. *"Go ahead and be angry. You do well to be angry*—but don't use your anger as fuel for revenge. And don't stay angry. Don't go to bed angry. Don't give the Devil that kind of foothold in your life" (Ephesians 4:26–27, *The Message*, italics mine).

It's okay to be angry. Let me repeat, it's okay to be angry. The feeling is not the problem; it's what you do with that anger that becomes sin. When you strike out in hatred and belittle and scorn the object of your wrath, cutting into the very core of who he is, then you have committed sin. In fact Jesus referred to it as murder, and the consequence is severe judgment.[5] The key is learning to be angry without hurting others.

And that begins by learning to admit you have this feeling. When my shoulders tighten, my teeth grit, my hands turn into fists, and that blackness begins to envelop me, I don't shove it away. Instead I acknowledge it. Just saying aloud that I feel angry right now does more to ease the pressure of it than stuffing it ever did.

2. Make friends with your anger.
Believe it or not, in the past several years, I've begun to welcome this feeling as a sign of something not quite right in my life and recognize it as an opportunity to learn something more about myself.

For example, persistent anger with someone at work led me to reevaluate my job. I decided that as good as this job was, what was most important to me were my relationships. So I looked for and found another job where I'm much happier. Another time I over-reacted to an off-the-cuff remark by my sister. In analyzing why, I realized that it was my old fear of appearing stupid. And when I looked closer at my irritation at Larry, I discovered my need to be in control.

Remember the man I mentioned earlier who comes into the public library where I work and views pornographic material on the Internet? His screen is in full view of other patrons, including children. My boss told me that there's nothing I can do about it since our policy is full access. I found myself filled with rage whenever he walked through our doors. I could hardly look at him, I was so angry. I prayed about what to do and played with all sorts of things that I could do to him, most of which would get me fired. Then one day he walked in and this thought came to me: *Judy, I love him as much as I love you.* It was so foreign to my thinking that I knew it was from God. Now when he walks in I pray for him and am con-templating inviting him to church. (When I told my boss this, she advised me that I couldn't do that either.)

I still don't like what he does, but I've come to realize that he needs the Lord as much as I do. God uses my anger to teach me lessons that I might not learn otherwise.

3. Identify your "triggers."

One way to get control of your anger is to become aware of what triggers it. Identifying these triggers will go a long way toward dispersing the angry feelings.

In almost every instance when I've stepped back and analyzed the event that ignited my anger, I've discovered another response that I experienced first—fear. One day my family went hiking in the mountains. Our destination was a small lake with a spectacular view. After a few hundred feet we discovered that several large boulders had slipped off the hillside and blocked the trail. I was ready to turn around and go back, but Larry and the boys decided to climb over them. I argued, begged, and pleaded, but they ignored me. I angrily stomped back to the car mumbling unkind things under my breath. When I got to the car and started to cool down a bit, I realized my anger was not from their ignoring my wishes, but from the fear of their falling off the steep hillside and into the river below. My first feeling was fear; my secondary feeling was anger.

My first reaction when Larry ignores me is fear that he's angry with me, and my second feeling is anger. When he talks to a pretty woman, my first feeling is jealousy (a form of fear); my second feeling is anger.

Another trigger is when I set a goal and it's blocked. For example, when I have a deadline and I'm pushing myself to finish an article, I am upset when the phone rings or the boys burst into the room or Larry wants me to help him find the checkbook. When bad traffic blocks my goal of getting to work on time, I glare at the other drivers and mutter unkind words.

Other triggers include people who treat me like I'm stupid, drivers who don't use their turn signal, library patrons who take advantage of the system, phone solicitors, and my cat when he's nagging me to feed him and I'm trying to knit—triggers are as individual as our fingerprints. They say a lot about who we are and what we want out of life.

Next time you get angry, try stepping away and looking at the situation. Look for the fear, the blocked goal, the unrealistic expectation, or whatever else triggered your ire. When you find it, you'll understand yourself a little better and begin to get a handle on your own feelings.

4. Take charge of your feelings.
We know that feelings are inner responses to outer stimuli. If this is true, then it follows that my husband doesn't give me anger. My

feelings come from my interpretation of events. Of course, it doesn't always feel that way, especially when he knows a certain action will provoke me. In those instances it seems that he's making me angry, but the source of the anger is still within me.

Something I used to love to do was stop for donuts after church. For some reason it just made my whole Sunday seem special whenever we'd do this. It was a treat for the boys, and it gave us a chance to visit and unwind after a busy morning. But Larry would never offer and I thought he should. As we drove out of the church parking lot, I'd wait and wait and wait for him to say something. Sometimes I'd pray he'd just stop for donuts as a surprise, but he never did. By the time we were a block past the donut store, I'd be seething. My whole Sunday would be ruined because I thought he was thoughtless and stingy and mean.

I got over this when I began to look at it differently. When we left church, he was thinking about what to do with the rest of his day. Donuts to him were no big deal, so he never gave them a thought. It had nothing to do with me. When I let go of my silly pride and simply reminded him, he was glad to stop and enjoyed our time together as much as I did. My anger was coming from my judgment of what he was thinking, not from reality.

It follows then that if I'm responsible for the feeling that's welling up inside of me, I can control it. Believe it or not, each of us chooses when to get angry and when not to. This may sound unreasonable because we often judge that we have no control, but the reality is we have more control than we want to admit. Sometimes I like to get angry because it makes me feel in charge. I like having people bow to my wishes, and if anger accomplishes that, then all the better. I know that attitude is sin. I know that it's not God's best for me. Admitting I have mastery over my anger means taking responsibility for my actions. I can't blame it on PMS, not enough coffee, or too much pressure, even though I want to. Taking responsibility for my actions makes me a better person not only at home, but also at work.

5. Deal with your anger as soon as possible.

One of the key statements in the Ephesians passage I quoted earlier is "Don't go to bed angry." I remember the first time I put this into practice. We were at a meeting with several other couples. Larry said something funny about my cooking. Everyone laughed and I joined in, but on the inside I was hurt. On the drive home I thought about not saying anything; after all, it was petty and not worth making a fuss over. I knew I was being overly sensitive and probably unreasonable. I argued with myself for several miles, but having just learned this principle, I knew I needed to practice it.

Going against my nature, I said, "Larry, what you said tonight hurt me and I feel angry."

To my surprise, he didn't defend himself or laugh at me. Instead he looked amazed, and then he apologized. He hadn't meant to hurt me, and I knew that, but I needed to hear him say it.

The rest of the drive home, we talked and held hands. By stating my feelings, we were able to clear the air, and instead of the remark keeping us apart, it actually drew us closer. If I hadn't said anything, the crack in our relationship would've been there until the next incident broke it open. It takes courage sometimes to break out of our "nice lady" rut and stand up for ourselves, but when we do, it can bring surprising results.

I think it's interesting that the next part of that scripture says, "Don't give the Devil that kind of foothold in your life." I think unresolved issues are dangerous. They fester inside like an infection and, if not treated, will spread to other parts of your relationship. You end up fighting over little things because the real issue is too touchy to handle. Facing issues head-on can be scary.

Money is one of those topics that I like to avoid. There never seems to be enough of it to go around for everything we need, let alone for the little luxuries that I want. I feel guilty if I buy something that I can't afford, and yet if I deny myself, I feel resentful. There have been many times I just took the bit in my mouth and did what I wanted to without consulting Larry. The result has been guilt. I wanted to talk to Larry about having some kind of allowance, but I feared that he'd talk budgets and point the finger at my recklessness. Keeping quiet seemed like the best solution, but this only led to resentment and more guilt, which led to more anger. I think you get the picture. But aren't we all guilty of this? If it's not money, it's sex or in-laws or discipline or drinking too much or a myriad of other things that get buried in long-term relationships. Yes, it's painful to talk about these issues, but settling matters will ultimately bring a lot more peace than burying them. Things may be a little uncomfortable for a while, but isn't that better than letting your spouse harm himself, your marriage, or your children?

Right now I'm in the market for a new computer. I've been shopping around, and yesterday I think I found what I wanted. My first impulse was to buy it and then tell Larry, but I knew that wasn't right. Last night I talked to Larry about it at length, and we discussed the pros and cons. He didn't tell me I couldn't get it, which was my fear. Instead he was supportive and helped me to talk through my decision. I don't know why it felt uncomfortable to bring up the issue, but I feel much better today than I did yesterday.

One of the issues we used to fight about all the time was his helping (or not helping) around the house. We used to go round and round about this, and he always promised to be more helpful, but it never translated into anything tangible. Then one day I analyzed what it was that bugged me. It came to me that just walking upstairs and seeing the bed unmade ruined my whole morning. So one day I simply asked him if he'd make the bed in the morning. It was a specific request, not some general "I need help." He agreed and now every morning he makes the bed. What a difference that has made in my attitude, and it's not much work for him either. If I'd simply buried my resentment, it would have continued to build year after year. This simple solution has worked for both of us, but it took some time to come to it.

What are the issues you avoid or continue to fight about? Some of them I know are as serious as addictions to gambling, alcohol, or drugs. But most of us are driven to distraction by daily things like work schedules, discipline of the children, watching sports on TV, spending money, and debt. Whatever your issues, ignoring them won't make them better.

6. Keep to the subject.

When you bury your anger, the result is often out-of-control fights. Once the dam has been broken, it's tempting to bring up everything else your husband has done in the past. But this is counterproductive. It inflates the fight and does nothing to resolve the issue.

7. Call for a time-out.

Sometimes I need time to process what I'm feeling, so I ask if we can talk about the issue later. Trying to understand what's going on inside of me in the middle of an argument leads to confusion and more anger. When I have the issue clear, then I can speak to it more calmly. Taking issues to God in my prayer time helps me get a new perspective that I would never have thought about.

If you do postpone a discussion, be sure and bring the issue up. Don't avoid it out of fear of making waves or starting a fight. Burying your anger is never a good option. You might think it's forgotten, but your stomach will keep track.

8. Pray.

When you're in the middle of a heated argument, sometimes the last thing you want to do is bring in God. Anger makes us feel in control, and praying reminds us that we are servants. But I have found that is exactly when I need Christ the most. I pray for my words, that they will be clear and kind. I pray for my tone of voice, that it will be soft and not hateful. Then I pray for logic, that I won't rely solely on my feelings. Last, I pray for my husband, that he will hear me clearly.

9. Listen.

Once Larry left me standing on a street corner in Richmond, Virginia. It was 95 degrees with 100 percent humidity. The worst part was that he drove right by me. I just stood on that corner staring as our little blue Pinto station wagon disappeared down the road. I was so angry I could have spit nails. I had been on my feet all day, and I was tired and hungry. When I finally got through to him on the phone, he was just leaving our apartment to go swimming. I blew up.

Every time I thought about this incident I got angry again. Years later, I realized that we had just miscommunicated. He thought I had another ride home, and I was sure we had made plans for him to pick me up. If I had listened first and held my anger awhile longer, I could have stopped a fight that took me years to forgive.

The passage in James says, "Everyone should be quick to listen, slow to speak and *slow to become angry,* for man's anger does not bring about the righteous life that God desires."[6] This is incredibly wise counsel, and if we followed it, many fights would never start.

10. Get angry.

This may seem like strange advice, but for those of us who are peacemakers, expressing our anger is almost impossible. Maintaining peace, at any price, seems like such a good thing to do, but it leads to shallow relationships and frustrations that never go away. You don't talk about anything that will help you have the marriage you desire because you're afraid to rock the boat. Divorce becomes the easy way out. Instead of speaking up for yourself or saying what you want, you manipulate or hint—neither of which most men understand.

Anger that's not expressed can turn into depression or an ulcer or headaches. I know because I have experienced all of these symptoms.

Sometimes getting angry is for the best. Recently we had just gone to bed when the phone rang. It was our son who's going to college in California. He was having a crisis, and I was trying my best to listen. Larry angrily told me to hang up and come to bed.

When I got off the phone, I had two choices: I could just ignore my anger or I could say something. The old me would have just gone to bed and lain there for hours fuming. But instead, I stuck up for myself and said something. We exchanged heated words, but in the end we made up and even felt closer to each other than before. When you bury your anger, it leads to a distancing and actually causes more damage than exchanging a few angry words.

Maybe you can't identify with burying your anger because you are a woman who expresses her anger openly and freely and you have found this effective in getting what you want. Harriet Goldhor Lerner in her book *The Dance of Anger* talks about being angry all the time. She concludes that neither burying anger nor letting it all hang out gets us what we want. She found that because she was always blowing up, no one listened to her; just as I discovered that all of my hinting and manipulating was getting me nowhere.

It's good to get angry, especially if your husband is treating you disrespectfully. Don't allow him to call you names or put you down. Stand up for yourself and tell him what you want in a straightforward manner. If he's hitting you, then get out of the home. Find a safe place for yourself until he gets help.*

Don't allow him to be destructive to those around you either. Stand up for your children.

If he's drinking or doing drugs, get help. Go to Alanon and learn how to deal with someone with an addiction. Don't justify wrong behavior because you are afraid of losing control.

If you don't like your marriage the way it is, then fight to change

* Call your local police department and ask for their domestic abuse advocate or call the National Domestic Violence Hotline at 1-800-799-7233.

it. I heard of a man who went for counseling after his wife left him. One day after their last child had left home, he came home and found her gone. He said he had no idea she was unhappy. This man may have been awfully dense, but part of me wondered why the wife hadn't told him that she was miserable. Why had she allowed him to behave this way? We can't force our husbands to change, but if we don't speak up and say what we want or need from them, we are depriving them of the possibility of change. And we are denying ourselves the possibility of a fulfilling marriage.

This man would've given anything to be given another chance, but his wife wasn't interested.

11. Toughen your hide.

For years I wore my heart on my sleeve. Any slip of the tongue, facial expression, or tone of voice that I perceived as criticism from Larry, and I'd let my feelings get hurt or I'd get angry and withdraw. I wouldn't bother to find out the truth, because my perception was more important than the truth. Larry had to walk on eggshells, pick his words carefully, and at times avoid me altogether in order to keep the peace. Of course, I saw him as weak for not standing up for himself.

You have to pick carefully what you get angry about. Make sure that it's something worth fighting for, not some perceived slight.

In Marriage Encounter we had rules for fighting. The one that has stuck with me all these years is: Don't hit below the belt, but don't wear the belt around your neck. Being overly sensitive and getting angry about every little off-the-cuff remark or sideways glance doesn't do anything to change your husband. It only creates tension in your home.

12. Learn to walk in forgiveness.

I recognize that God has forgiven me, and I offer that same, moment-by-moment forgiveness to my husband. I treat him the way Christ treats me. I give him grace. He can be thoughtless, uncaring, and even rude, but then so can I. Letting him be angry and irritable and loving him anyway has been an incredible growth step for me. I've been able to do it because God has granted me the same grace.

When you learn to forgive, you will discover that your anger will slowly disappear and you will find the peace that God has promised.

❧

Action item: Think about the way you handle your anger. Do you withdraw, attack, or deny? Write out a plan to behave differently.

CHAPTER TWELVE

I Married the Wrong Man

*For I am persuaded that neither death nor life, nor angels nor princi-
palities nor powers, nor things present nor things to come, nor height
nor depth, nor any other created thing, shall be able to separate us
from the love of God which is in Christ Jesus our Lord.*
ROMANS 8:38–39, NKJV

*I*f you are not already involved in an extramarital affair, you may
have contemplated the idea. This is one of the ways women try to
escape marital situations they deem impossible.[1] On the surface it
looks like the answer to your problems. Someone new will love you
the way you've always wanted; he will take away your loneliness, the
primary cause of affairs,[2] and give you a safe, secure haven to run to
when you leave your current husband. But is this the answer?

When I met my husband, I was dating someone else. He was
tall, blond, and a good dancer, the three most important elements
in a man when you're nineteen. There never was anything serious
about the relationship, but when I told him I was marrying Larry,
he suggested that if I waited we would get married. I was flattered

but decided to go ahead with my plans. That should have been the end of it, but it wasn't.

A few years into our marriage, out of boredom more than anything, I began to fantasize about this man. I wondered where he was, what he was doing, whether he ever thought about me. I eagerly greeted any word about him. When my marriage began to fall apart, I spent even more time thinking about him and imagining all sorts of scenarios. I started looking for him in crowds and even looked up his phone number.

Was this wrong? How can my living, breathing, less-than-perfect husband live up to a memory of someone whom I hardly knew? He can't. My imaginary lover doesn't leave his socks on the floor, grind his teeth at night, ignore my tears, act interested in me only when he wants sex, watch TV instead of talking to me, or walk out in the middle of a fight. He can be anything I want him to be: a good listener, a fantastic lover, romantic, selfless, thoughtful, and kind. I was being disloyal to my husband by thinking and dreaming about another man in an inappropriate way.

According to Frank and Bunny Wilson, authors of *The Master's Degree—Majoring in Your Marriage,* "Infidelity starts when a person allows her mind and emotions to drift to a person other than her spouse."[3] That is exactly what I was doing. Instead of thinking positive things about my husband and learning to accept him, faults and all, I was comparing him to someone he could never live up to. And as the years went by, my discontent only grew. I have come to call this behavior an "Affair of the Mind." It may have relieved my boredom and filled my lonely hours, but it led to nothing but discontent within my heart.

Imagining that there is someone out there whom you just haven't met yet is another form of an Affair of the Mind. You might be thinking that your present spouse obviously isn't the right one, or you'd be happy and content. Our current culture has popularized the idea that we all have a true soul mate who will fulfill our every need. Is this true? Once you said, "I do," your husband became the "right one." Believing there is someone else out there is a big mistake that does nothing but erode your present satisfaction with your husband.

Most of the good men are already married, and many of those who are left have been divorced at least once. Second marriages aren't stronger because people have learned from their mistakes. On the contrary, they are more likely to fail and in a shorter period of time.[4] Dreaming about a future meeting with Mr. Right is about as logical as planning on winning the lottery.

Another form of an Affair of the Mind is comparing your husband to characters in books and movies. Remember that someone has carefully crafted these men from their imagination. They are not real and, even if they were, they probably wouldn't make good husbands. Think about Rhett Butler in *Gone with the Wind,* Mr. Rochester from *Jane Eyre,* or Max DeWinter from *Rebecca.* These men are all dark and mysterious and just a wee bit dangerous. They make great fictional material, but in day-to-day living, they would be impossible to live with.

Jesus understood how precious the bond of sexual and emotional intimacy in marriage is. That is why in Matthew he says, "But I say to you that whoever looks at a [man] to lust for [him] has already committed adultery with [him] in [her] heart."[5] Jesus was more concerned with the condition of the heart than with the outer appearance, and he understood that many of the people he was talking to were guilty of Affairs of the Mind. Once you allow someone else to enter that private world that should only belong to you and your husband, you've destroyed or at least damaged what binds you together.

Are you having an affair? An article that appeared in *Psychology Today* cited three elements that determine whether a relationship is an affair:[6]

1. Secrecy. You meet or talk with someone of the opposite sex and you feel you can't tell your husband. This includes conversations over the Internet or through the mail.

Marilyn is a runner. She met Bob at a local gym, and they began jogging together every morning. He was good looking and younger than she was. She didn't think her husband would understand, so she never told him about their daily meetings.

2. Emotional intimacy. "When someone starts confiding things to another person that they are reluctant to confide to their partner, and the emotional intimacy is greater in the friendship than in the marriage, that's very threatening. One common pathway to affairs occurs when somebody starts confiding negative things about their marriage. What they're doing is signaling: 'I'm vulnerable; I may even be available.'"[7]

Patricia met Jim in a chat room on the Internet. She was surprised how easy it was to "talk" to him. She found herself looking forward to their conversations and began confiding in him her secret dreams that she'd never told anyone, not even her husband.

3. Sexual chemistry. "That can occur even if two people don't touch. If one said, 'I'm attracted to you,' or 'I had a dream about you last night, but, of course, I'm married, so we won't do anything about that,' that tremendously increases the sexual tension by creating forbidden fruit in the relationship."[8]

Susan had always thought of Ralph as a nice guy. They worked together in the same firm and exchanged good-humored insults. Then one day, Ralph told her he was attracted to her. Since both were married, they agreed that it could go no farther. Now Susan can't get Ralph out of her mind.

Whether your infidelity happens in the past, present, or future, it can do great damage to you and your marital happiness. It also may hurt those you're closest to. Your children may be more likely to commit adultery.[9] It may ruin your reputation and destroy most if not all of your friendships. It will damage your testimony and your relationship with God. There is nothing we as Christians can do to fall out of God's love,[10] but our sin affects our relationship with him. He doesn't move, but because of our own guilt and shame, we separate from him. It is only when we have a clean heart that we know he's hearing our prayers. You will carry the guilt with you the rest of your life, and it will cause you to destroy your relationship with your spouse.

June was surprised when she fell in love with a man she worked with, because she truly felt she was also in love with her husband. She thought she could love both of them, but she soon found herself being more and more critical of her husband. Simple flaws became big issues, and she found herself looking toward the day when she would divorce her husband and marry the other man.

But is this likely to happen? If the other man is married, the answer is probably no. Only a small percentage of men who get involved in an affair leave their wives. That's probably because for men affairs tend to be about sex, while women tend to think they're about love.[11]

Even if you do leave your husband and marry this person, consider that he's a home wrecker. If he strayed once, he may stray again. And what about you? Can your new husband trust you? What guarantees can you give him that you won't stray again? The chances are good that your affair has more to do with your neediness than with love.[12] One woman I know was attracted to a man because he touched her gently, another because he treated her like she was intelligent, a third because he just paid some attention to her. All of these are legitimate needs, but getting them met in this way is not the answer.

Exchanging partners may feel good for a while, but once you've settled down, you'll discover that you have the same marriage all over again.

If you're not already involved in an extramarital affair, here are some things you can do to avoid having one:

- Don't confide in anyone of the opposite sex, even in writing. The most innocent "friendships" need boundaries.
- Don't flirt.
- Try not to be alone with someone of the opposite sex. If meeting them alone, even for business purposes, invite a third party along. I've had several professional women tell me that this is ridiculous in today's business world, but my advice still stands. No one, even a professional woman, is immune to an affair.
- If you feel yourself looking forward to being with someone more than your husband, cut the relationship off. Don't give explanations, just stop seeing or talking to that person.
- When you find yourself thinking about someone in an inappropriate manner, stop your thoughts immediately. Prayer is a good thing to do at this point. Or think about something positive in your husband.
- Tell someone you are attracted to another man. Part of what drives an affair, even one of the mind, is the secrecy. When you tell, that diffuses this aspect. Virginia was attracted to one of her students. She was embarrassed and ashamed and vowed never to tell anyone. After struggling with her feelings for quite a while, she finally got a handle on them when she told her husband. The light of truth is the only thing that will make the dark of sin leave our minds.
- Never tell the other person that you are attracted to them. This will only feed the emotional intimacy.
- When you feel a sexual attraction for someone, admit it to yourself and take appropriate steps to avoid that person. The worst thing you can do is deny the attraction, because then you become an accident waiting to happen.

If you're currently involved in a sexual affair:

Ask God for forgiveness. Now is the time to develop an honest and open relationship with God. Bear your soul to him and then ask his forgiveness. "If we confess our sins, he is faithful and just and will forgive us our sins and purify us from all unrighteousness."[13]

Pray that the Lord will restore your relationship with your husband. Pray that he will take the desire out of your heart and guard you against future sin. Put on God's armor. Spend daily time in prayer and meditation on the Word. Go to church and get involved with other Christian couples. Avoid movies and television shows that celebrate adultery.

Memorize the following scripture: "Finally, brethren, whatever things are true, whatever things are noble, whatever things are just, whatever things are pure, whatever things are lovely, whatever things are of good report, if there is any virtue and if there is anything praiseworthy—meditate on these things."[14]

Flee. Depending on how emotionally involved you are, this may be the hardest step of all. Your affair is filling a need, and maybe for the first time in your life you are feeling as if you are in love. This is Satan's greatest deception. He knows if he can get you to believe this, then he has you hooked. However, the Bible says, "The heart is deceitful above all things, and desperately wicked; who can know it?" (Jeremiah 17:9, NKJV). We can't trust our feelings. They will lead us astray just as surely as they led David to sin with Bathsheba and Bill Clinton to sin with Monica Lewinsky. The only possible solution is to cut the affair off immediately.

The Bible uses the strongest possible language when it says, "Flee sexual immorality . . . [she] who commits sexual immorality sins against [her] own body. Or do you not know that your body is the temple of the Holy Spirit who is in you, whom you have from God, and you are not your own? For you were bought at a price; therefore glorify God in your body and in your spirit, which are God's."[15]

I think it is interesting that following Jesus' statement on adultery in Matthew, he says, "If your right eye causes you to sin, pluck it out and cast it from you; for it is more profitable for you that one of your members perish, than for your whole body to be cast into hell. And if your right hand causes you to sin, cut it off and cast it from you; for it is more profitable for you that one of your members perish, than for your whole body to be cast into hell."[16]

Does this mean that you need to cut off part of your body? No, but it does mean that it is better to quit your job, ask for a transfer, move to another department, change churches, or do whatever else you need to do in order to avoid this person. When things were bad in my marriage, I began flirtatious relationships with two men at work. They would stop by my office and visit several times a week. I don't think they meant anything harmful, but I began to want more. These relationships became very uncomfortable. When the opportunity arose, I applied for and got another job. I left a job I liked rather than risk getting involved.

Stop and evaluate. Consider that your "lover" may not be what you want in a husband. I know three women who were involved in affairs. One man had been married five times before, the second was in this country illegally, and the third had no means of support other than his wife. Remember, the physical attraction and the sneaking around have clouded your thinking. Step back and look at this person objectively. Is this someone you want to live with the rest of your life? (If your answer is yes, reread chapter 2.)

Get counseling. After you end your affair, run to your nearest counseling center. I suggest a biblical counselor who can guide you through the healing process. You have cut off an important relationship, and you will go through a mourning process just like a death. The closer the relationship, the more pain you will endure. But isn't it better to suffer for a little while than to hurt everyone around you? Don't expect healing to happen quickly. It will take time. A good counselor can help you walk through the process.

"And the God of all grace, who called you to his eternal glory in Christ, after you have suffered a little while, will himself restore you and make you strong, firm and steadfast."[17]

Discover the root of the problem. Dave Carder, author of *Torn Asunder: Recovering from Extramarital Affairs,* says, "The affair is an artificial world spun together by the [adulterer] in an attempt to have [her] gnawing emotional deficits addressed."[18] Once you discover the deep need the affair is filling, then you can do something about it. Most affairs are an attempt to fill a need for love.

I was exposed to pornography at an early age, one of the common backgrounds of people who commit adultery, as cited by Carder. Other factors include too strict a childhood, parents who abused drugs or alcohol, sexual molestation, or a history of affairs in the family of origin.[19]

Consider telling your spouse. Carder highly recommends confessing.[20] This might be good for you in order to rebuild intimacy in your current marriage. Let a counselor help you decide if this is best and when you should do it.

Guard against recurrent adultery. According to Carder, once you've committed adultery, unless you take care of the underlying reason, you will probably recommit.

Finally, ask yourself this question: Am I using this affair as an excuse to leave my marriage? Statistics remind us that 84 percent of women who have affairs go on to divorce their husbands,[21] but only 15 percent of people who leave for this reason actually get married.[22] Think about that. The man you are seeing now may not want to marry you after you leave your husband. What will you do then? Or perhaps you're just using this other person to give you the courage, or an excuse, to leave. Is that fair to him?

Real or imagined, as long as you are having an affair, there is no hope that your marriage can truly be all that God intended it to be. If you truly want to restore your marriage, then you will have to get rid of your fantasies.

I know this from firsthand experience. I fell in love with someone whom I never would have believed I would be attracted to. The relationship started out as friends, but then one look and just like the romance novels describe, it was like being struck by lightning. It seemed as if he'd crawled right into my skin, and I couldn't get him out of my mind. Lies filled my head and I believed he was my "soul mate," my "one true love," my "other half." I thought that without him I could not possibly be happy. Even though we never even held hands, leaving my husband felt like the right thing to do. Staying went against everything my heart ever wanted. I knew I should cut off the relationship, but I couldn't stop seeing or talking to him. I thought my life would end if I did.

I heard a well-known pastor say that he'd had an affair like this. It was the most difficult thing he'd ever gone through because the roots went so deep and were incredibly hard to remove.

Stopping this relationship was the most difficult thing I've ever done, but the pain I suffered was nothing compared to the agony that my husband, children, family, friends, coworkers, and church would have gone through if I hadn't. The question that's even harder to ask is, What would I have done to the reputation of Jesus Christ?

I didn't leave. I stayed and rebuilt a relationship with my husband. It's stronger than ever and deeper because of what I went through.

If I had left, I think that one day I would have written a letter similar to the one that appeared in my local paper.

Dear Ann Landers,

I'd like to share my story because I know a lot of people think of their lives the way I thought of mine.

Sometimes you feel lonely and unloved in a marriage—even after 23 years. You feel as if there's got to be more to life, so you set out to find someone who can make you blissfully happy. You believe you have found that someone and decide he is exactly what you want. So you pack up and say goodbye to your 23-year marriage and all the friends you made when you were part of a couple. You give your children the option of coming with you or staying with their father.

You live the glorious life for a few years, and then, a light bulb goes on in your empty head. You realize that you have exactly the life you had before—the only difference is that you've lost your friends, your children's respect and the best friend you loved and shared everything with for 23 years. And you miss him.

You realize that love doesn't just happen, it must be nurtured through the years. You cannot undo what has been done, so you settle for a lonely and loveless life with emptiness in your heart.

Ann, please print my letter so others won't give up something that is truly precious—and let them know that they won't know how precious it is until they have thrown it away

Heavy-Hearted in Philly[23]

Don't throw away what you have for another man. Work on your marriage relationship and find what you're looking for in it. When I look at my children and see how well they're doing, and I cuddle up in the evening with my husband, I praise God that I stayed.

I'd like to share with you one of the scriptures that got me through this ordeal: "He will cover you with his feathers, and under his wings you will find refuge; his faithfulness will be your shield and rampart."[24]

Action item: If you are having a real or imagined affair, ask for God's forgiveness, and make a plan to stop it right now.

CHAPTER THIRTEEN

ℐ Don't Want Him to Touch Me

Therefore a man shall leave his father and mother and be joined to his wife, and they shall become one flesh. And they were both naked, the man and his wife, and were not ashamed.

GENESIS 2:24–25, NKJV

𝒮ex. Nothing has given such pleasure or caused as much pain. The message from the world is that it's as easy as falling off a log. You just do it, and everything works like clockwork. In the movies, clothes disappear magically. Elbows, knees, and toenails are never an issue, and timing is perfect. In reality there are buttons and zippers and clasps that get stuck. Body parts poke and jab and scratch at the most inopportune times and timing takes practice.

When I married, I thought sex was going to be the experience that would bring me total fulfillment. All the longing in my heart would be whisked away by a single act, and I would finally feel loved, complete, and beautiful. From watching the movies, I determined that sex was the answer for everything. No matter what was wrong with a relationship, slipping under the covers would solve the problem. Sex to me was the ultimate in intimacy. The melding of our bodies would bring about some magical melding of our souls.

And that seemed to be true for a while. It was fun and exciting and I looked forward to every encounter. Giving myself so completely was wonderful, and afterward I felt warm and loved. I was always ready, no matter how tired I was or how bad my day had been.

But somewhere along the way, I changed. Sex, instead of being a want-to, turned into another have-to. And I resented and dreaded it.

I often look back and wonder when my attitude changed. Was it the year that Larry, due to a lot of stress in his life, didn't want me at all? Was it my way of defending myself against the pain of rejection? No book, sex education, or girl talk had prepared me for this possibility, and I heaped much of the blame on myself. I felt unfeminine, fat, and ugly. I stared in the mirror and wondered what was wrong with me. To ease the hurt, I steeled myself against desire.

Did I change out of fear of getting pregnant? Two babies less than two years apart took away my feeling of control over my body. Worry about birth-control failure haunted every encounter.

Was it during the years that I worked full-time and was so tired that I often cried because I couldn't get everything done? Many nights I fell into bed totally exhausted and dragged myself up in the morning dreading another day.

Was it worry over the boys bursting in on us unexpectedly and the feeling that we'd lost all privacy?

Or was it the way Larry changed? He seemed only interested in me when he wanted to make love. The rest of the time, he treated me as if I didn't exist.

Whatever the reason, sex became a chore and I resented it. When I said no, I felt guilty, and when I said yes, I felt resentful. I was caught in a bad dream with seemingly no way out.

If you, too, struggle in this area, then I want you to know I don't have any magical key or Bible verse to help you. Our problems are as individual as we are. Perhaps you are married to a man who wants sex three times a day or never. Perhaps you were sexually abused as a child or raised in a family where you were taught that sex was a bad thing. Maybe you've had multiple lovers or an abortion. Maybe you've been raped. All of these things bring up a whole lot of issues that I have no quick answers for.

What I do know is that sex is not simply a physical act. It somehow binds two people together in an almost magical way that can't be explained by mere human minds. In Genesis it says, "They became one flesh." The physical act somehow blends two into one and transcends the mere act itself. Did you know that humans are the only animals that have sex face to face? God had something more in mind when he created sex than just a way to reproduce. It was a way to bind two people together.

This is reflected in the fact that healthy marriages seem to have healthy sex lives. I know that the best years of my marriage have been the ones that were filled with playful sex, eagerly anticipated by both of us, on a regular basis. There is nothing more wonderful than giving myself to Larry with abandon and having him receive my gift as something precious to be cherished.

Effective communication is an imperative for a successful sex life. Learning to talk about this topic with your husband will do more for you than any book or seminar. However, this can be scary. There is probably no other area of our lives where we feel so vulnerable. To expose our hidden desires or deepest needs to another person is like running down the freeway naked. Here are a few helpful lessons I've learned about this subject.

Take an attitude inventory. Before you can communicate with your husband on this subject, you need to look deep inside yourself and determine what you believe about the sex act. Do you believe it was invented by God or by someone in a back alley behind a porno shop?

When I was about ten or eleven, I was exposed to pornography. I knew it was wrong because we sneaked the magazines behind the adults' backs. Seeing pictures of nude women gave me a guilty thrill. (These mental images are still with me today.) It opened me to feelings that I wasn't ready to handle and gave me erroneous ideas about sex. The hesitation of the adults in my life to discuss this topic with me and the way everyone snickered when a dirty joke was told left me with the impression that sex was dirty—something nice girls would never do.

The truth was I could hardly wait to do what was forbidden and had many sexual fantasies. But after I married, I never thought I could share them with Larry. What would he think of me? And so for a big part of my life, I hid. I couldn't bring myself to discuss with him what felt good and what didn't. I expected him to know. He was older and more experienced in so many areas, I assumed sex was one of them—even though I knew I was his first and only sexual partner.

Later, much later, I learned he was probably even more naive than I was. We both had a lot to learn. If we hadn't been so reticent to discuss sex, our problems could have been remedied much earlier.

When I first heard that God actually designed us for sex and that he said it was good, I was incredulous. Whenever we made love, I closed the door so the children couldn't see and so God wouldn't know. To invite him into our bedroom was unthinkable.

One weekend, we left our kids with a sitter and drove north a few miles to a motel. After a nice dinner we returned to our room and began making love. But there was a problem. The music that was being piped into our room was from a Christian radio station. Strains of "Amazing Grace" and "In the Garden" weren't exactly my idea of romantic. I tried to block it out of my head, but couldn't. I was just about to stop everything and turn it off when I remembered that what we were doing was okay and part of God's plan for us. And so I began to pray. The result was that for the first time I experienced sex without shame and guilt. It was tremendously freeing.

My belief that sex was dirty damaged our relationship more than any one thing. Learning that it is a good, healthy part of marriage freed me not only to experience it, but also to talk about it with Larry. I shared my likes and dislikes and my fantasies, and instead of being disgusted he was pleased. Our sexual relationship has blossomed because I was willing to do this. It is now much more satisfying for both of us.

Accept your body. How do you view your body? Are you pleased with the way you look or are you ashamed? We women have a hard time with this. What is portrayed as beautiful in society today is hard to live up to.

Did you know:

- There are three billion women who don't look like supermodels and only eight who do?
- Marilyn Monroe wore a size 12?
- If Barbie were a real woman, she'd have to walk on all fours due to her proportions?
- If shop mannequins were real women, they'd be too thin to menstruate?
- The average American woman weighs 144 pounds and wears between a size 12 and 14?
- One out of every four college-aged women has an eating disorder?
- The models in the magazines are airbrushed—they're not perfect!
- A psychological study in 1995 found that three minutes spent looking at models in a fashion magazine caused 70 percent of women to feel depressed, guilty, and ashamed?

- Models who twenty years ago weighed 8 percent less than the average woman, today weigh 23 percent less?

No one has a perfect body. Learning to accept the way you look can go a long way toward making you feel comfortable in the bedroom. But if you don't feel comfortable, then let your husband know how you feel. Larry likes seeing my naked body, but I still have to fight those natural feelings of modesty that God gave me. I feel uncomfortable when I'm naked, and letting Larry know that helps him to understand my reticence.

Chart your physical desire. During your menstruation cycle your hormones fluctuate, which causes your physical desire to go up and down. I find that just before I begin menstruating, my desire goes up. Just after I ovulate, my desire is at its lowest. Knowing this has helped me relax and understand that part of what I'm feeling (or not feeling) is physical.

I've shared this with several friends, and they've told me that their desire peaks at different times from mine. Every cycle is different. Learn yours and then take advantage of your peaks. And don't get discouraged during your off times.

Get in touch with your feelings. Because of past abuse, you may never want to feel any sexual desire again. Many women have cut themselves off from these sensations. Whether you know it or not, your body will respond to certain stimuli. Getting back in touch with these feelings will be hard, but it can be done. Look for the physical signs: breast enlargement, lubrication of the vaginal area, and swelling of genitals.[1] Practice giving in to them and letting yourself feel the physical sensations of arousal. At first this may be hard, but little by little the feelings will return.

Make an appointment. Now that you know some things about yourself, it's time to talk to your husband. Pick a place away from the bedroom, such as a restaurant where the seating allows you to talk privately. (Other suggestions are taking a walk, driving in the car, a romantic bed-and-breakfast without TV or phones, or any place where you can be alone together.) Pray for God's wisdom as you speak to your husband. Be assured he will give you the words. Practice good communication techniques and keep everything positive. Speak about your wants and desires, not what your husband is doing or isn't doing. Be honest, but not destructive. Keep your emotions out of it and don't go on and on. Say what you want to and then be quiet. Listen to your husband's reply carefully. Try to be as receptive to him as you would like him to be to you.

Let him know your goal is to improve this part of your relationship, not to condemn. This may take several sessions. My best advice is to keep them short.

Read a book together. If talking about sex seems impossible or uncomfortable for either of you, then I have another suggestion. Try reading a book together. One of the best things my husband and I did was read a book about sex. Once or twice a week we would go to bed, and one of us would read a chapter out loud. This broke down barriers and gave us permission to talk about some rather sensitive and even embarrassing topics. Even though we'd been married several years, we learned a lot about each other's bodies. The reading opened doors to discussions that never would've happened naturally. If you'd like to try this, I would like to recommend Clifford and Joyce Penner's *The Gift of Sex.* It's an honest look at sexuality from a godly perspective. Other books that are available are Ed Wheat's *Intended for Pleasure* and H. Norman Wright's *In Touch with Each Other.*

Create a private language. It's important to be honest with your husband about what you like and what you don't like, but bringing it up in the middle of a romantic interlude can be disastrous and can easily be misinterpreted as an insult. We've created our own language that tells the other one what's happening without interrupting the moment.

Part of our code involves using a scale of one to ten. This has been invaluable, and we've learned to use it in all sorts of ways.

When Larry is getting romantic and I'm not sure I want to go ahead, I will ask him if he's a ten. If he says yes, then I know how badly he wants to make love, but if he says he's a five, then I know that I can say, "Why don't we wait," without causing any problems. I can also tell him that I'm a two, which reminds him that he needs to slow down, so I can catch up with him.

We also use the comparison of the iron and the light bulb. Sometimes Larry thinks I'm not interested because I'm not as ready as he is. I gently remind him that I'm an iron and it takes time for me to warm up. His response is like a light bulb, and he's ready to go when the switch is turned on.

Our private language includes the example of a boxcar and a spider web. When Larry is ready to make love, it's like he has entered a separate boxcar. He can shut everything out of his mind and concentrate fully on the task at hand. My mind is more like a spider web. I'm aware that we're making love, but I'm also aware that I have laundry waiting, a friend whom I forgot to call, a bill that needs to be paid, and a deadline looming. My mind can be wandering all over the place and distracting me. All I have to do is tell him my spider web is getting in the way, and he knows that he needs to make an adjustment in our lovemaking. By talking to me, he helps me concentrate.

Be honest. When faced with the dilemma of whether or not to say no or yes, be honest first with yourself and then with your husband. Give yourself permission to say no. If you honestly don't want to make love, then say so. This may be a good time to talk to your husband about what's going on inside of you. You may discover a different kind of intimacy.

Be willing to compromise. There are times I don't feel like making love, but I do it anyway. Why? Because I think it's what is best for my marriage and what God wants me to do and what is ultimately best for me. I hesitate to use this scripture because it has been misused so many times, but I think there's a wonderful truth contained in it.

The wife does not have authority over her own body, but the husband does. And likewise the husband does not have authority over his own body, but the wife does. Do not deprive one another except with consent for a time, that you may give yourselves to fasting and prayer; and come together again so that Satan does not tempt you because of your lack of self-control. But I say this as a concession, not as a commandment.

1 CORINTHIANS 7:4–6, NKJV

Look carefully at what Paul is saying. He's not saying we have to make love when we don't feel like it or that our husbands have the right to abuse us in this area. He's saying that we have mutual control over each other's bodies. This means we must respect each other's needs and desires. And then he says this is not a command. We don't have to.

But if I want to do what is best for everyone, I give myself like a gift. I do the same every day in a million little ways. I give, expecting nothing in return, out of love for my God. He never has asked me to do anything that wasn't within my ability and wasn't the best for me.

We get things all mixed up down here on this sinful earth. We become centered on self. Christ came so that we could get our eyes off ourselves and find real happiness in giving to others.

Sex is a gift. And when given, something wonderful is given in return. I might not be in the mood to begin with, but as I relax and give in to Larry's gentle caresses, I soon discover I am as eager as he is. John Gray in his book *Mars and Venus in the Bedroom* says, "It is through sex that a man's heart opens, allowing him to experience both his loving feelings and his hunger for love as well. Ironically, it is sex that allows a man to feel his needs for love, while it is receiving love that helps a woman to feel her hunger for sex."[2]

But, you say, your husband wants sex three times a day and once a week is enough for you. A friend described it as eating a Thanksgiving meal topped off with pumpkin pie and whipped cream. Afterward she's stuffed and doesn't need to eat for a long time. Her husband, on the other hand, thought of sex as a snack that only whetted his appetite for more. These two might be the extreme, but in most marriages different sexual needs are normal. Dr. Deborah Newman in her book *Then God Created Woman* says, "In every marriage, someone is having sex more often than he or she wants, and someone is having sex less often than he or she would like. In good marriages, couples compromise and are able to give and receive in order to satisfy both partners."[3]

Sexual desire fluctuates not only during your menstrual cycle, but through the different stages of life.[4] The amount of sex that I desire now that my children are grown is much different from when they were toddlers. It's also different from when we were first married, and I know it will be different as I approach menopause. Just as I go through different stages, so does my husband. There are times in his life when he isn't as interested as I am. As things change in your life, so will your desire. Accepting this as normal, and learning to put your marriage first, will go a long way toward making you content in this area.

Get a physical. If sex is painful or uncomfortable, then see your doctor. This is not normal. You may have a physical reason for this discomfort that can be easily remedied. If you are not totally happy with the type of birth control you are using, then this would be a good time for discussion. It took several tries before we found the right combination that worked for us.

Sex doesn't have to be a battleground in your relationship. It can be a place where you can find intimacy.

SEXUAL INTERCOURSE IS IMPORTANT

It relieves tension. When Larry and I go for a period of time without making love, tension builds between us. We become testy with each other and sometimes explode over little things. Regular sex lowers the stress level in our relationship. This was borne out in a study of 37,500 adults. "People with fulfilling sex lives were found to be less anxious, violent and hostile, and not as likely to blame others for their misfortunes."[5] Sexual intimacy is good for you in other ways too. The hormones that are released during sexual intercourse fight depression, help with the immune system, and decrease heart attacks.[6] In one study it was even found to relieve the symptoms of PMS.[7]

It keeps you and your husband from sexual impurity. When we're not satisfied at home, we may be attracted to another person more easily. This can be true for both marriage partners.

It creates intimacy. Giving yourself to another in this way develops intimacy. It means making yourself vulnerable and involves a high level of trust. We go away at least once or twice a year to be alone. The sexual intimacy leads to a closer intimacy in all areas of our relationship.

God designed sex. Ed and Gaye Wheat in their wonderful book *Intended for Pleasure* wrote: "You have God's permission to enjoy sex within your marriage. He invented sex; He thought it up to begin with. You can learn to enjoy it. . . . If your marriage has been a civil-war battlefield or a dreary wasteland, instead of a lovers' trysting place, all that can change. You see, God has a perfect plan for marriage, which we may choose to step into at any time, and the mistakes of the past can be dealt with and left behind."[8]

May I suggest that you make a date right now with your husband for a sexual interlude? I used to think this was a sacrilege. For sex to be good, doesn't it have to be impromptu? *No.* If you wait until you feel like it, especially when you have small children or busy lives, you probably will seldom get around to it. Great sex can happen even when you plan for it. You can get a baby-sitter for the evening or take the kids to Mom's house for the weekend, and get away.

Does that sound expensive? It doesn't have to be. We put our small change into a jar. At the end of the year we have saved enough for a night in a hotel and a nice meal out. Look for free offers and discounts. Learn where there's an inexpensive place within a short driving radius and make it your place. Go there at least once a year. I know of someone who has discovered a getaway that has no phones or television.

Prepare yourself. Buy a new nightgown or perfume. Take a bubble bath or shower together. Pamper yourself and your mate. Maybe a foot or back rub would help one or both of you relax. Many hotels now have hot tubs that can help ease your tension.

Making the effort to improve your sex life will pay rich dividends.

♋

Action item: Make a date with your husband tonight for a sexual encounter this week. Plan it carefully.

CHAPTER FOURTEEN

I Don't Feel Loved

Jesus loves me this I know
For the Bible tells me so.

How many times have you sung this verse? Do you believe it? Truly, down in your heart, believe it? I have been a Christian for most of my life, but I have to admit this is hard for me to grasp. How can a holy and righteous God love me? He sees into my heart and knows the wickedness that is hidden there, and yet the Bible says he loves me. How can that be?

When I was eleven a new girl moved into our small town. Her name was Kay Gish. She had dark hair and freckles and a smile that lit up the room. I liked her immediately, but so did everyone else. Never in my wildest dreams did I believe she would be my friend. I was shy and gawky. I didn't stand out in any way. I never won a spelling bee or a footrace. No one ever picked me first when selecting teams or asked me to be the star in the school play. Kay on the other hand was graceful and beautiful and just about perfect in my estimation.

To my surprise, she called and asked me to come over and we became friends—best friends even. She didn't have to pick me, but she did. When I think about that time, I'm still amazed that she thought I was someone special. That's pretty much how I feel about my relationship with God. He could have anyone in the world, and yet he chose me.

His love is more real to me than most of the people who populate my life. But it hasn't always been that way. For years I treated God like Alka Seltzer. I kept him on a shelf and only pulled him off when I needed him. He played no part in my day-to-day living, and I didn't even give it a thought when I married a non-Christian. (Larry became a Christian when he was twenty-nine.) But when a crisis appeared or I needed something important, I readily, almost automatically, turned to God. There was the time Larry had his tonsils out, and I thought he was going to die from the surgery. When I found out I was pregnant and the doctor told me I probably wouldn't carry this child past the first trimester, I pleaded with the Lord to save my baby. I also turned to him when I wanted something, like my internship or our new house or my first job. Other than that I never let him affect my life much at all.

My relationship with God changed after Larry accepted Christ and we started going to church. I rededicated my life, and at first I felt as giddy as a new bride. Six months later our marriage started to fall apart, and that joy disappeared. Even after we renewed our commitment to one another, I never felt the joy and happiness that I saw reflected in other people's faces. Jesus said that his burden was light,[1] but for me his burden was heavy. I felt like a whole set of rules had been dumped into my life that only made me feel more like a failure than ever. Billy Sunday summed it up when he said, "The trouble with many [women] is that they have got just enough religion to make them miserable."[2]

That is an accurate description of me. I was miserable, and yet I kept reading in the Bible that my faith would make me happy and loved and fill my life with joy. *What a joke,* I thought at the time. I was tempted to walk away, but I couldn't somehow.

I had just enough faith and experience to understand that what I was looking for was to be found in my relationship with Christ and nowhere else. C. S. Lewis said it best in *A Grief Observed:* "You never know how much you really believe anything until its truth or falsehood becomes a matter of life and death to you. It is easy to say you believe a rope to be strong and sound as long as you are merely using it to cord a box. But suppose you had to hang by that rope over a precipice. Wouldn't you then first discover how much you really trusted it? . . . Only a real risk tests the reality of a belief."[3] It's easy to believe something when you feel like it. It becomes a real test when you decide to believe when you don't feel like it. I decided to trust my rope with my future happiness; I decided to trust what the Bible said: "Ask and it will be given to you; seek and you will find; knock and the door will be opened to you. For everyone who asks receives; he who seeks finds; and to him who knocks, the door will be opened" (Matthew 7:7–8).

I determined to test this rope. I read books, listened to Christian speakers, studied the Bible, prayed, and became involved in ministry. Slowly, like one door opening into another, I found what I was looking for. My discovery began with getting rid of what I call my "stinking thinking." These are firmly held false beliefs that affect our relationships profoundly. In order to discover your own "stinking thinking," answer the following questions. Be honest, don't give intellectual responses. Search your heart until you know the truth, then answer. Write your responses someplace where you can refer to them easily. Ask God to reveal your heart.

1. Do you believe you are lovable? If so, name those you love unconditionally. Do you feel you can truly be yourself with your friends, relatives, and spouse, or do you put on a "show" to impress those around you?

2. How do you view God? Look at your relationship with him

and describe it fully. How does it differ from your relationship with your earthly father?

3. What fear(s) keeps you away from God? These might include the fear of changing, the fear of what others might think, the fear of what he might ask you to do.

4. What do you blame God for? Search your past and see if there is something that you are angry about that you blame God for.

Do You Believe You Are Lovable?

When I looked in the mirror, all I could see were my imperfections, which in my view far outweighed my good points. I saw a woman who'd rather stay home on Sunday morning, read the paper, drink coffee, and watch a football game than go to church. I saw someone who occasionally read a book or watched a movie God would not approve of. I saw a woman who forgot to iron her husband's shirts; she ate the wrong things and rarely exercised; her furniture needed a good dusting, and sometimes she let people down; she neglected her parents and purposely didn't return a call to a friend. I saw a woman who got angry and said hateful things to her husband and children. She didn't measure up to her own standards; how on earth could she measure up to God's?

This feeling of not measuring up caused a dilemma. I wanted to be loved, but in order to be loved I had to let people get close to me. But if I let people get close to me, they might discover my imperfections. My stinking thinking told me that no one could love an imperfect person like me. The pain of not living up to people's expectations was too much for me to bear. My answer was to build a wall of protection. I thought it kept people and God from discovering my shortcomings, but it also kept me isolated and alone. At church I put on my Christian smile, even though I was struggling in my marriage and with my faith. When my friends or neighbors dropped in, I showed them my latest sewing project or bragged about my children's good grades or offered them homemade cookies, hoping they wouldn't notice my deep unhappiness or that my carpet needed vacuuming. When family came to visit, I talked about my newest purchase or latest writing project or what brilliant children we had produced, hoping they would think everything was fine, when it wasn't.

Another aspect of this stinking thinking was that I assumed no one wanted to spend time with me. When my neighbors called to invite me over for lunch or a cup of coffee, a small voice in the back of my head told me that they were only being polite. I turned down invitations to go shopping or to the movies, believing that the person didn't want me along. I even suspected that my mom and dad and sisters and brothers only came to visit out of a sense of duty and because they liked my husband and wanted to see our children. Conversely, I seldom called anyone or asked them out to lunch or into my home.

I found fault with Larry, hoping to take everyone's eyes off my own shortcomings. I assumed he didn't love me either. When he focused on a TV program or the newspaper or buried himself in the garage, I judged it was just further proof that he didn't care about me.

Just as this stinking thinking affected my human relationships, it also affected my relationship with God. I couldn't believe that God could love me any more than the people who populated my life. I filled my head with knowledge of him, but I never let it touch my heart. I filled my life with rules to keep, but I never accepted his grace or his love.

I worked hard to earn God's love. I went to church, studied my Bible, took lay-witness training, memorized scripture, prayed, tithed, joined a women's group, and cleaned communion cups, but it wasn't enough. I judged that I always fell short. My Christian walk, instead of bringing the joy that is talked about in the Bible, brought me just another list of things I had to do and be in order to feel loved. I felt more burdened each time I failed to measure up.

During that time if a non-Christian had walked up to me and asked, "Why should I become a Christian?" other than for salvation, I would not have had a good reason. Nothing that I had experienced up to that point gave me anything to recommend to a friend.

In the midst of my struggle, a Christian speaker said something that began a process of discovery: "The reason you don't feel loved, is that you don't feel lovable. You were born with a hole in your heart that may never be filled, but that doesn't mean you aren't loved."

I shared this with a friend and she suggested I read the following psalm. I posted it on my refrigerator and read it every day:

O Lord, you have examined my heart and know everything about me. You know when I sit or stand. When far away you know my every thought. You chart the path ahead of me, and tell me where to stop and rest. Every moment, you know where I am. You know what I am going to say before I even say it. You both precede and follow me, and place your hand of blessing on my head.

This is too glorious, too wonderful to believe! I can never be lost to your Spirit! I can never get away from my God! If I go up to heaven, you are there; if I go down to the place of the dead, you are there. If I ride the morning winds to the farthest oceans, even there your hand will guide me, your strength will support me. If I try to hide in the darkness, the night becomes light around me. For even darkness cannot hide from God; to you the night shines as bright as day. Darkness and light are both alike to you.

You made all the delicate, inner parts of my body and knit them together in my mother's womb. Thank you for making me so wonderfully complex! It is amazing to think about. Your workmanship is marvelous—and how well I know it. You were there while I was being formed in utter seclusion! You saw me before I was born and scheduled each day of my life before I began to breathe. Every day was recorded in your Book!

How precious it is, Lord, to realize that you are thinking about me constantly! I can't even count how many times a day your thoughts turn towards me. And when I waken in the morning, you are still thinking of me! . . .

Search me, O God, and know my heart; test my thoughts. Point out anything you find in me that makes you sad, and lead me along the path of everlasting life.

PSALM 139:1–18, 23–24, TLB

I read and reread this verse so many times that I memorized it, but still I couldn't bring myself to believe that God loved me for who I was. Oh, I believed it on an intellectual level, but it took a long time to penetrate my heart.

WHAT IS YOUR VIEW OF GOD?

Many women have a problem with the image of a loving heavenly Father because of their relationships with their earthly fathers. Susan shared with me that she had spent her whole life trying to earn her father's attention and love, but had failed miserably. Everything she did was never quite good enough. She longed to hear him say, I love you and am proud of who you are, but he never did.

Other women struggle because their fathers physically or sexually abused them. Others can't accept the concept of a loving heavenly Father because their father was absent due to work, divorce, illness, or addictions. The image of a loving father isn't easy for many of us to comprehend, and yet that's how he loves us. Whether we feel like it or not, whether we acknowledge it or not, whether we go to church or tithe or study our Bible, he loves us. When we cry he longs to take us into his arms and soothe our pain and stroke our hair. "You have seen me tossing and turning through the night. You have collected all my tears and preserved them in your bottle! You have recorded every one in your book" (Psalm 56:8, TLB).

He's warm and personal, kind and accepting, encouraging, and, best of all, he's always there for us. He's the perfect love relationship that we've been longing for all our lives.

How you view God can greatly affect your relationship with him. I saw him as cold, distant, and busy. He lived way off in heaven somewhere and, with a few million people to watch out for, was much too busy to be bothered with my petty needs. I also viewed him as demanding and judgmental with a long list of expectations that I could never live up to.

The concept of a loving heavenly Father just wasn't real to me. When I prayed, it was as if I were talking to myself. I couldn't imagine that God had time to listen to me, and even if he did, I thought he dismissed my prayers as unimportant. I never turned to him when I needed a shoulder to cry on. I truly thought he'd just say to me, "Stop your blubbering, or I'll give you something real to cry about."

An elder in our church says that when we are hurting we should climb into God's lap and let him hold us, just like a daddy. I couldn't grasp that kind of love. I was strong and independent. My favorite motto was "do it myself." All of my relationships were at arm's length, and I was uncomfortable with people who wanted to get too close to me. The kind of relationship he described scared me. It meant I would have to be vulnerable before God and expose the good, the bad, and the ugly. But the Bible clearly says, "And I ask him that with both feet planted firmly on love, you'll be able to take in with all Christians the extravagant dimensions of Christ's love. Reach out and experience the breadth! Test its length! Plumb the depths! Rise to the heights! Live full lives, full in the fullness of God."[4]

The love Paul is describing is similar to the love we feel when we first fall in love or when we hold our newborn babies. We can't keep our eyes off the object of our love. We think about them day and night, and everything we do is for them. That's how God loves me; that's how God loves you!

If it isn't a wrong image of God that is keeping you away, perhaps it's something else even more stinking; perhaps it's fear.

WHAT FEAR(S) KEEPS YOU FROM A COMPLETE RELATIONSHIP WITH GOD?

I teach an adult Sunday school class. This is how the women responded to this question.

They feared they would have to change. We might not like everything about ourselves or be as happy as we'd like, but we have become comfortable with who we are. Change is scary.

The Bible says: "Take your everyday, ordinary life—your sleeping, eating, going-to-work, and walking-around life—and place it before God as an offering. . . . You'll be changed from the inside out. . . . God brings the best out of you" (Romans 12:1–2, *The Message*).

They feared they would be asked to do something uncomfortable. We might have to go down to Skid Row and feed the homeless or visit someone in the hospital or go visiting for the church on Tuesday nights. As scary as those things are, what if God asked us to become a missionary to Uzbekistan or Honduras? We might have to live in primitive surroundings and give up everything we now enjoy like warm baths, comfortable beds, shopping malls, and fine restaurants.

The Bible says: "Self-sacrifice is the way, my way, to finding yourself, your true self. What kind of deal is it to get everything you want but lose yourself?" (Matthew 16:25–26, THE MESSAGE).

They feared they might have to give up their possessions. Remember the rich young ruler who was told that all he had to do was give his riches away to the poor in order to become a follower of Christ? What if God asked us to do the same?

The Bible says: "You're blessed when you're content with just who you are—no more, no less. That's the moment you find yourselves proud owners of everything that can't be bought" (Matthew 5:5, *The Message*).

They feared what others might think of them. We all grow up hearing comments from friends and relatives about those crazy religious nuts. It's acceptable to believe, but not to make others uncomfortable. I recently heard a politician say that in the United States it's now more acceptable to be called a perjurer than a Christian. Most people don't want to be thought of as radical. We all want to belong, to fit into our peer group. Being a totally sold-out Christian is not acceptable.

The Bible says: "There's no telling who will hate you because of me. Even so, every detail of your body and soul—even the hairs of your head!—is in my care; nothing of you will be lost. Staying with it—that's what is required. Stay with it to the end. You won't be sorry; you'll be saved" (Luke 21:17–18, *The Message*).

They feared they would have to give up their enjoyable habits. Let's face it. We all have habits that keep us from a close relationship with Christ. Maybe you smoke, read racy romance novels, like a glass of wine, go to the races, do a bit of gambling, or live with a boyfriend. You know these things are wrong, but you don't want to give them up; and you definitely don't want someone making you feel guilty about them.

The Bible says "It's what God does with your life as he sets it right, puts it together, and completes it with joy. Your task is to single-mindedly serve Christ" (Romans 14:17, *The Message*).

They feared life would become dull and uninteresting. Once you have to give up all the fun stuff, then life will become a bore and all you will be able to do is sit around home and read the Bible and go to church. Heaven even sounds dull. Who wants to sit around all day singing and playing a harp?

The Bible says: "Let the heavens rejoice, let the earth be glad; let the sea resound, and all that is in it; let the fields be jubilant, and everything in them. Then all the trees of the forest will sing for joy" (Psalm 96:11–12).

I am a sports fan. Every now and then I get to go to a University of Washington football game. I have been a part of an audience that's standing and cheering as the quarterback makes a last-minute pass that was caught in the end zone for the winning touchdown. As exciting as that was, I don't think it even begins to compare to what we will experience in heaven.

At church our worship leader sometimes asks us to welcome the Lord Jesus Christ into our midst. We give him a standing ovation, and I am filled with awe as I think about what it's going to be like to see him enter a room, to touch him, to hear him speak. I don't think this will be dull.

I also don't think we'll be sitting around playing harps all day. I think we each will have a special gift that we will use, whether it be painting, singing, or teaching. We won't be idle. We will be doing exactly what we've always wanted to do.

Dull? I don't think so, not for a moment.

WHAT DO YOU BLAME GOD FOR?

An older woman whom I know has been angry at God for eighty years because an uncle who was a well-known evangelist didn't speak to her at her father's funeral. Another woman went through a terrible divorce and the pastor at their church seemed to care more about her husband who had molested her children than about her. When I was a teenager, a man in my church whom I regarded highly did something that I considered hypocritical, giving me a good excuse to put God on a shelf. Perhaps it was the death of someone close to you or a child that was born with a birth defect or a disaster that changed your life forever. Maybe it's the relationship you're in now. Maybe you feel God lied to you because things aren't working out between you and your husband.

When my marriage started falling apart and I prayed for God to fix it and he didn't, I grew angry and resentful. How could God love me and not fix my marriage? Church became a torture; I hated all those smiling faces and happy greetings. Slowly I withdrew from all activities. Just as my relationship with my husband was deteriorating, so was my relationship with God. I couldn't go to church and face the reality that I wanted to divorce my husband.

ARE YOU A CONSUMER OF LOVE?

Consumers are needy people. At their very core they don't believe they are lovable. And yet that is what they want more than anything. And so they go around trying to earn everyone's love. They are the obedient children, the ones who never do anything wrong, the ones who never rebel or make waves. They go through life with empty, leaky hearts looking for someone who will love them enough to make them feel loved.

I lived my whole life looking for people to love me. I did what I thought they wanted so that they would like me. My motive was selfish. I gave love only to get love. The problem with this way of living is that no one can make you feel loved. It's like trying to fill up a leaky urn. Because my need was so great, my very life depended on what others thought of me. And I failed miserably. I was unable to be all the things I needed to be to feel loved.

THE ANSWER

I knew the answer was to be found in my faith. I could see it in the faces of my friends, hear it in the voices of the choir, and read about it in scripture. "Though you have not seen him, you love him; and even though you do not see him now, you believe in him and are filled with an inexpressible and glorious joy."[5] "I have told you this so that my joy may be in you and that your joy may be complete."[6]

"But the fruit of the Spirit is love, joy, peace, patience, kindness, goodness, faithfulness."[7]

These scriptures spell it out clearly; all of the things I longed for were at my fingertips, but I couldn't find them and was so frustrated.

I, who never asked anyone for help, began inquiring of my husband, friends, and others about how I could find these feelings. A total stranger gave me the final piece to my puzzle. She said, "You don't feel God's love because you're looking at him all wrong." I knew she was right. That night I could hardly sleep for thinking about this. I was struck by how I'd lived all my life with an intellectually wrong view of God. The next morning, I sat on my couch and with fear of being struck dead told God how I'd thought of him as cold and distant and uncaring. I sobbed as I realized that it was my wrong thinking that was the barrier between us. I pleaded with God to forgive me for all of my stinking thinking. "I just want to feel your love, God; I want to know your joy; please, God, fill my heart with you."

There were no lightning bolts, no visitations by angels, and no music filled the air. I got up from that couch not feeling much different from when I had sat down, but slowly, during the days and weeks that followed, I began to notice a change. My heart felt lighter, and every once in a while this unexplained joy bubbled up inside of me. I laughed out loud at a robin trying to pull a worm out of the ground. My heart would fill with delight at the way my children smelled when they came in from playing outside. I couldn't help the happiness that welled up inside of me at work after finding just the right book for a child. I had more energy and eagerly looked forward to every day. Instead of a consumer of love, I became a giver. Instead of feeling sorry for myself because no one ever asked me to lunch, I made the first move and invited others to go eat with me. I made it my goal every day to make the people I came in contact with feel the love of Christ. I found good things to say to my coworkers, the angry person who came to the desk to check out books, my husband, my children, and my friends. I sent notes to let people know I was thinking of them. I phoned to just say hello to my sisters.

As I allowed God to fill my heart, I got my eyes off myself and focused more and more on others. I lived this scripture: "Here is a simple rule of thumb for behavior: Ask yourself what you want people to do for you; then grab the initiative and do it for *them*! . . . Help and give without expecting a return."[8] Instead of worrying about others not loving me, I made it my goal to help others feel the love that now swelled up inside of me. I wanted them to discover their own unique gifts and learn to accept themselves as God did. It was as if my heart overran, and I had to give it away.

I was no longer threatened when a friend didn't return my phone call. When my husband said something that I judged unloving or unkind, instead of letting my feelings be hurt, I forgave him the moment he said it. When my parents didn't write, instead of feeling ignored, I wrote to them. When my friends didn't call, instead of thinking they didn't care about me, I called to let them know I cared about them. When my husband seemed distracted, instead of assuming he was angry, I asked what he was thinking. I was able to love my children even when they weren't lovable. It was a miracle.

The loneliness that I had felt all my life melted away. Being with God was like spending time with my very best friend. I told him everything that was in my heart. I let him fill me with his forgiveness and love. Instead of being afraid of changing, I asked him to change me. I looked for ways that I could grow.

And he has never asked me to do anything that I didn't desire with all my heart. Before I was serving him in ways I thought were what he wanted but they were not what I wanted. But I learned that serving God is to do exactly what you always wanted to do. A missionary to Uzbekistan told me that when God calls you to be a missionary you can't imagine doing anything else, and he fills your heart with an unexplained love for the people of that country. Serving becomes a joy, not a burden.

Has your stinking thinking kept you away from the love that you've always wanted? If you get nothing else out of this book, I hope and pray it is this one thing. No matter what decision you make about your marriage, nothing will impact your life more than this.

My dear children, let's not just talk about love; let's practice real love. This is the only way we'll know we're living truly, living in God's reality. It's also the way to shut down debilitating self-criticism, even when there is something to it. For God is greater than our worried hearts and knows more about us than we do ourselves.

And friends, once that's taken care of and we're no longer accusing or condemning ourselves, we're bold and free before God! We're able to stretch our hands out and receive what we asked for because we're doing what he said, doing what pleases him.

1 JOHN 3:19–20, *The Message*

God took a scared housewife who was afraid of her neighbors and thought she had no real friends and turned her into a woman whose life is filled with wonderful women who love me more than I ever believed possible. He has taken the two things I feared most in my life, writing and speaking before groups, and caused me to long for the opportunity to write and speak. It truly feels like a miracle. And the effect it has had on my relationship with my husband has freed me to love him and accept him because I feel loved and accepted. I can see his faults and love him anyway because God loves me.

He's turned my life into something special, and he can do the same for you. Martin Luther said, "It is not that you have value and therefore God loves you; God loves you, and therefore you are valuable."

Philip Yancey in his book *The Jesus I Never Knew* tells of a woman who gave him this incredible advice: "Let God love you." I want that to be my advice to you. Sit back, stop working so hard, and simply let God do the work. Let him love you.

I challenge you to trust God. Take the Bible at its word. Live the abundant life he has promised.

❧

Action item: Read the following every day for a week:

Love knows no measure
but is fervent without measure.
It feels no burden, it shirks no labor.
It desires more than it may attain.
It complains of no impossibility, but it thinks
that all things may be done for its beloved.
Love therefore does many great things
and brings them to completion,
whereas the one who is not a lover faints and fails.

Love wakes much and sleeps little,
and sleeping sleeps not.
Love faints, but is not weary,
is restrained in its liberty, and yet knows great freedom.
It sees reasons to be afraid, and fears not.
Like a quick brand or spark of fire,
it flames always upwards by fervor of love unto God,
and through the special help of grace
is delivered from all perils and dangers.

The spiritual lover knows what it is to say:
you, Lord God, are my whole love and desire.
You are all mine and I am all yours.
Gather my heart into your love that I may know
how sweet it is to serve you,
and how joyful it is to please you.

I shall sing to you the song of love.
I shall follow you, my beloved,
wheresoever you go,
and my soul shall never be too weary to praise you
with the joyful song of spiritual love
that I shall sing to you.

I shall love you more than myself
and myself for you.
I shall love all others in you and for you,
as the law of love commands
which is given by you.

—THOMAS À KEMPIS[9]

CHAPTER FIFTEEN

I Just Want to Be Happy

The supreme happiness of life is the conviction that we are loved.
VICTOR HUGO, *LES MISÉRABLES*, 1862[1]

*S*omething marvelous happens when we finally realize that we are loved—it sets us free. Jesus said he came not to condemn the world (for all our failures) but to free the world. "This is how much God loved [you]: He gave his Son, his one and only Son. And this is why: so that no one need be destroyed; by believing in him, *anyone can have a whole and lasting life.* God didn't go to all the trouble of sending his Son merely to point an accusing finger, telling (you) how bad (you are). He came to help, to put the world right again" (John 3:16–17, *The Message*, italics mine).

He didn't come just to give us eternal life, but to help us live full, happy lives right here, right now. How? By accepting that we are who we are. God created you. God created me. He didn't make a mistake. He knows our names and calls us beloved.

What is our job then? *To become fully who God created us to be.* Not what our parents want us to be, not what our husband wants us to be, not what some book says we should be, but who we really are.

When I first grasped this, it was like turning on a light in a dark room. I had been living in the dark. I thought that if I was beautiful and thin, did everything right, and achieved modest success, then I would be loved. But God loves me totally and completely just as I am. All he wants is for me to become wholly me.

Most of us don't know who we are. We've chosen paths in our lives for the wrong reasons. We go to college because it's expected, we choose careers because they pay well or will give us prestige or make our fathers or mothers proud. We take jobs because we think that's all we can get or deserve. We choose mates based on hormones or what others think or because we're pregnant and getting married seems like the right thing to do. (I've had more than one woman tell me they married their husbands because they didn't think anyone else would ever ask.) We have all made mistakes because we don't know ourselves, we don't appreciate the freedom we have in Christ, we haven't taken time to evaluate our lives, and we haven't taken responsibility for ourselves.

GET TO KNOW YOURSELF

I urge you to learn who you are and what you want out of life. You may need to turn the TV off, put aside the novel you're reading, say no to someone, or take a day off from your busy schedule. To some of you taking time to reflect may seem wasted, but how else will you ever get to know you? Go to the park, the library, or just sit on your couch. Take out a piece of paper and begin to write.

First, write the word *talents*. Now list yours. Do you enjoy working with people? Are you artistically or musically gifted? Do you like to cook or sew or decorate? Perhaps you're good at organizing or maybe you'd rather follow. I am creative and no matter what I do for a living, I will create. My favorite part of my job is designing a colorful, eye-catching bulletin board every month. I also knit, quilt, and of course write, not just nonfiction, but fiction too.

If you're not sure of your talents, make a list of the things you enjoy doing and see what they have in common. Look back at your childhood and ask yourself where you excelled. Several writers that I know wrote poetry and stories as children and were highly praised by their teachers. But as they grew older, they got sidetracked into careers like engineering, nursing, and teaching.

Perhaps you loved art, horseback riding, dance, or music, but you put those things aside when life got in the way. The woman who cuts my hair grew up loving music. In her thirties she picked up her French horn and now plays in a community orchestra and performs in musical productions.

The wife of a man I work with has started offering dance lessons and performing in local musical theater. A coworker has gone back to school to pursue a degree in interior design. My own sister received her civil engineering degree in her forties.

Maybe your talents are hidden. I would never have dreamed that someday I would be a writer. In school I excelled in science and avoided classes that required writing. A teacher never told me that I had a gift. In fact, whenever a paper was assigned I could pretty much depend on a B or C grade. And yet at age thirty-five, I discovered that was exactly what I wanted to do.

Do some searching; take some classes; volunteer at church, a local museum, the library, or your child's school. Search until you find something that you absolutely love to do. Then pursue it. It is probably what God created you to do.

Second, write "spiritual gifts," and list them. If you don't know what they are, seek out a pastor and ask him to give you a spiritual gifts test. Then imagine ways you can use your gift in ministry. So many of us believe that the only jobs available to women are teaching children in Sunday school and singing in the choir. This isn't true. There are numerous opportunities that you probably haven't considered. Ask your pastor what the needs of the church are. Perhaps they're in data processing, administration, organization, counseling, counting money, greeting, designing the Sunday bulletin, flower arranging, or phone calling. The only limit is your imagination.

One of the best things that Larry and I did was to become active in marriage ministries. In the process of helping other couples, we learned how to make our own marriage stronger. Things that I thought I could never accept about my husband became insignificant and even endearing as I saw other couples struggle with the same issues. This involvement led to Larry's decision to go into the ministry and my desire to write this book and speak to women.

Third, write "blessings" and make a list. God is so generous, but we often don't notice because we're so busy living or see only the negative. What is good about your marriage? What do you like about your husband? Search for the good, and you will find it. This may be hard at first because negative thinking becomes a habit and like most habits is hard to break. Every day we need to look for God's blessings. Maybe it's the sunrise or the snow on the mountains or, for us who live in the Seattle area, sunshine. Maybe it's the hug of a child, the smile of a store clerk, a pat on the back for a job well done, or a driver who lets us into traffic. Blessings don't have to be big things.

I remember taking my three-year-old cousin to the zoo. We wanted to show her the giraffes and bears and monkeys. But she didn't even notice them. What excited her were the squirrels, pigeons, and ducks that roamed freely through the park. I urge you to become like this child; look for the things that are under your feet, and begin to praise God for them.

GET TO KNOW THE FREEDOM YOU HAVE IN CHRIST

Satan's biggest lie is that we are victims of our circumstances. We think things like, *I am the way I am and I can't change; I have to work; I have to stay in this marriage; I have to go to church every Sunday; I have to keep my house clean; I have to . . .*

God came to set us free from all of our have-tos. He even gave us the choice of whether or not to believe in him. He has a light touch in our lives because he knows that love that is forced is not love at all, it's slavery. And so God gave us the greatest gift he could bestow, free will.

During my tenure on a job that I hated, I dreaded going to work every morning. I lived for the weekends, but then every weekend was ruined because I knew I'd have to go back to work on Monday. I wanted to quit, but Larry was out of work, and I was our sole breadwinner. The pressure to stay in that job was unbearable, and many nights I cried and begged Larry to let me quit. I had convinced myself that there was no escape, but I *could* have quit. You see, God takes care of us. He's there to provide for our needs. It's Satan's lie that we are caught in situations that we can't change.

You don't have to live your life like that. You can choose.

Every moment of every day, we choose. We choose whether or not to get out of bed. We choose whether or not to go to work or to make breakfast for our families. We choose whether to smile at that angry look from our husbands. We choose whether to be happy. We choose. It's when we start to believe we have no choice that we become unhappy.

I once owned a horse named Ginger. She was sweet tempered and easy to handle, until you tied her to a post. Once she realized she couldn't move about freely, she pulled back, and when she couldn't get away, she panicked. She jerked her head and reared and fought until she broke her rope. Isn't that how we are? We will take any confinement, until we start to wonder if we can't get away. When we pull back and meet resistance, we panic. And then if we believe we are caught and there's no way out, we become miserable.

Because I've walked in your shoes, I'm willing to wager a bet. Part of your unhappiness is that you believe you are trapped. That confinement is making you unhappy. It's not just what your husband is doing or isn't doing, it's your fear that you will have to live the rest of your life caught in this unhappy marriage.

But that's not true. At the risk of being misunderstood, I'm going to say something very controversial. You can leave.

A woman I know who is struggling in her marriage said to me one day, "But if I leave, God won't love me anymore."

I said, "Yes, he will. There is nothing you can do to make God love you less."

Her eyes opened wide. I know she didn't expect that answer from me. "Then why should I stay?" she asked.

"Because it's what's best for you," I answered.

The Bible says God hates divorce because he knows it's not the best answer for you, for your children, or for your husband. God loves us so much that he gave us the free will to choose whether to stay or not.

During those years when love seemed so far away, every day when I got out of bed I chose to be married one more day. Even when things looked bleak and I thought there was no possibility of my marriage changing, I chose to stay, to work, and to be loving. It was hard; there were days I wanted to pack my bags, but there were rewards along the way. Perhaps a friend would call to say hello, or I'd watch my husband carry our son to bed (even when he was almost too big to lift), or our family would laugh together as we decorated our Christmas tree. God gave me sunsets, snow in the mountains, a white Christmas, and a dogwood tree. It had been in our backyard for years, but we didn't know it until it bloomed one year. God used that dogwood tree as a confirmation that I was doing the right thing. He blessed me with a home that all the neighborhood kids flocked to after school for popcorn and Kool-Aid. Most of all he gave me two boys whose laughs touched my very soul.

On your paper, write "Have-to." Now make a list of areas in

your life where you feel trapped. Circle the traps you've created yourself and begin to make a plan to free yourself from them.

EVALUATE YOUR LIFE

Have you ever considered that part of your unhappiness may be coming from something other than your marriage? On your paper, write "Responsibilities." Divide this into three groups: daily, weekly, and monthly. Now list everything you do in a typical day, week, and month. Examine each item you listed and ask: "Would I be happier if I gave this up?"

If you work full-time, maybe you need to quit and go home to raise your kids. One of the best things I did for myself was finally quitting my job as a dietitian. Our income was cut in half, but God provided. We did without a lot of "extras" like dining out at expensive restaurants, microwaves, VCRs, vacations, new clothes, and fancy cars. Instead I sewed, made meals from scratch, and drove an old pickup. We didn't have much, but I was happier than I had ever been. I had energy and time to play with my children and teach them the things that I thought were important. I learned that quality time happens when you are there to take advantage of it.

During this time, we visited some friends who had children about the ages of ours. Both parents worked. We were there to see their beautiful new home. They also showed us their big expensive TV, their motor home, and pictures of their trip to Disneyland. On the way home, I looked at my boys sitting in the backseat and wondered if they were resentful that we didn't have all that stuff. And so I asked, "We could have all that they do, if I worked. Would you like that?" They both resoundingly said, "No." They wanted me at home.

If you have to work and you are unhappy, maybe you could find another job. Maybe it's not the work you're doing, but the relationships you're in. One of the things we do when we're unhappy with someone at work, especially a boss whom we can't communicate with, is bring it home and take out our feelings on our mates.[2] If there's no way you can quit, then work on your attitude. Ask how you can make your job better. Volunteer to take on new tasks or extra training. Do the work, even the boring stuff, as if you're doing it for the Lord. You know those icky tasks that no one likes to do, like cleaning out the office refrigerator or filling the ink stampers? Take the initiative to do them without being asked as a gift from God to those you work with. You'll be surprised how this changes how you view them. When you can't change your situation, ask God to help you accept it and to find the good side. It may take time, but he will answer your prayers.

Have you thought about a part-time job? That's what I finally did after my boys got to be teenagers. We needed the extra money, and I needed the social outlet. It took me several tries before I found the right one. I let other people know that I was searching and kept my ears open. All of my jobs came because someone I knew told me about the opening.

Now look at your list and circle the activities you resent. Ask yourself why you do them. Are you making a lunch for your husband every morning because that is what your mother did or his mother did? Are you secretly resentful because you hate to make them? Making his lunch is not a loving deed, if by doing it, you end up feeling angry. I turned over lunch-making to my husband. I just make sure the refrigerator is full of things he likes.

Are you making a big meal in the evening thinking that's what you should do, when in reality you hate it? Perhaps you can make a light meal or have ingredients ready that everyone can throw together when they want. This will be far more loving than doing something you resent.

A great solution for cooking if you work comes from my sister-in-law. She formed a group of women into a co-op. They take turns cooking for one another. One night a week they prepare enough food for four families. They then deliver the meal to one another's homes. This way each of them only has to cook one night a week.

Does all that housework weigh you down? My sister is an elementary-school teacher with three active teenagers. She has someone who comes in and cleans every Friday afternoon. She told me that this has changed her life. She used to come home Friday night and be depressed about how messy her home was. All day Saturday was spent cleaning when she really wanted to do other things. Now she comes home to a clean house. The happiness that she feels makes the extra expense worth it.

I discovered another convenience that has made my life easier—laundries. Every week I used to wash three or four of my husband's dress shirts that then needed to be ironed. Because I was so busy, I'd let them pile up until my husband was desperate. Then I'd spend a couple of hours ironing. Even though Larry was really patient and understanding about this I felt guilty, and that pile of shirts seemed to always be hanging over my head. Then I discovered that a local laundry will wash and iron them for less than a dollar each. My husband loves the way they look and has even taken over the responsibility of taking and picking them up.

Don't completely stop doing housework and cooking. Part of loving your husband is taking care of household responsibilities. Again, not because you have to, but because you know it's what God would want of you. If you can't do these things for your husband, then do them for the Lord. Do them happily. And you'll find a big difference in the way you feel about these jobs.

But no one ever says thanks, right? Why do we expect the people in our lives to be thoughtful and other-centered, when we aren't? When I find myself at this pity party, I look at myself and ask, How am I doing in this area? When was the last time I thanked my husband for going to work or mowing the lawn or taking out the trash? These kind of convicting thoughts always make me humble. Remembering my own ingratitude enables me to forgive my family, especially my husband, for never saying those wonderful words we all long to hear—thank you.

Now write on your paper "Health Issues." How are you feeling? Do you have frequent headaches, heartburn, or stomachaches? Are you getting enough sleep and exercise? Are you eating right? Do you cry often? Are you tired all the time?

I suffered from depression for fifteen years and didn't know it until I came out of it. Maybe the unhappiness you're feeling is a result of this ailment. Depression affects twice as many women as men.[3] Statistics show that more than one in five of us will fall victim to depression in our lifetime.[4] You could be suffering from this malady since an unstable marriage has been cited as one of the reasons for depression.[5] The symptoms include:[6]

- Significant weight gain or loss.
- Loss of pleasure in formerly enjoyable activities.
- You can't fall asleep at night, or you wake up repeatedly throughout the night.
- You sleep too much.
- Fatigue or loss of energy.
- Feelings of hopelessness, worthlessness, guilt, or withdrawal.
- Inability to concentrate or make decisions.
- Recurrent thoughts of death or suicide.

If you have experienced five or more of these symptoms every day for more than two weeks, then you probably are depressed.[7]

Today there are many resources for help. Seek out a good Christian counselor. With her help you can determine if you need to see a doctor who can prescribe medication. I know that there are some Christians who think that depression is a spiritual problem, but research has shown that there is a physical side to this condition.[8]

You wouldn't deny someone glasses if they couldn't see clearly, or an aspirin for a headache. I regret that I didn't get help sooner. I think about all the years that I wasted, when help was so readily available.

Are you getting enough sleep? Experts say that most of us need about eight hours every night, and that lack of sleep can make a big difference in how we feel.[9] Here is a list of symptoms (put a check by the ones you experience frequently):

- You need an alarm clock in order to wake up at the appropriate time.
- It's a struggle for you to get out of bed in the morning.
- You feel tired, irritable, and stressed out during the week.
- You have trouble concentrating.
- You have trouble remembering.
- You feel slow with critical thinking, problem solving, or being creative.
- You often fall asleep watching television.
- You find it hard to stay awake in boring meetings or lectures, or in warm rooms.
- You often nod off after heavy meals.
- You often feel drowsy while driving.
- You often sleep extra hours on weekend mornings.
- You often need a nap to get through the day.
- You have dark circles under your eyes.

If you suffer from more than three of these, it's a pretty good indication that you need more sleep. This alone can make a big difference in how much you enjoy life.

Other possible medical problems that can affect your emotional state include postpartum depression, hyperthyroidism, migraine headaches, PMS, menopause, or a myriad of other conditions. Simple solutions may be eating right, getting regular exercise, or losing a few pounds. But before you do any of these things, I strongly suggest a complete physical. Don't suffer needlessly.

TAKE RESPONSIBILITY FOR YOUR OWN HAPPINESS

For years I tried to make other people responsible for my happiness. I thought I'd be happy if:

- My husband was happy.
- He would only be more loving, make more money, take me places, shower me with presents, and help around the house.
- My children would behave, not fight, pick up their toys, get good grades, or be the star of the baseball team.
- My sisters and parents would write.
- My friends would call.
- My coworkers would carry more of the load, get to work on time, and do what was right.
- The sun would shine.
- We had a bigger house, newer car, or took fancy vacations.

I even blamed God. The truth is there is only one person who can make me happy—me. James 4:2 tells us: "Yet you do not have because you do not ask" (NKJV).

I can't make anyone do anything. The only person I have control over is me.

Something I learned from my sister as I watched her go through a nasty divorce was to do something nice for myself every day. This doesn't mean that you are being selfish. It means you are treating yourself like someone who is loved and deserves good things. If you are waiting for someone else to do something nice for you, you might wait a long time. Take a warm bath, shop for the little things that mean so much to you, like scented soaps, perfume, or a book. I enjoy fresh flowers, so I often buy a bouquet for my dining-room table. This feels extravagant, but one glance at a vase of daffodils or tulips cheers me up. Don't deny yourself the simple pleasures of this world.

However, don't do things or make changes that might involve someone else without thinking it through carefully. If I stopped work, brought home a free cat, had another baby, or stopped bathing, Larry would be affected. For these types of changes, you need to learn to ask. Don't manipulate, just come right out and say, "Honey, I would like to quit work." Then be quiet. Don't nag, don't bring it up a hundred times, don't leave notes around the house, don't push. Instead, pray. Let God work in your husband's life. It may take time, but when God answers your prayers, it'll be in the right time.

I have a friend who prayed for years that her husband would become the spiritual leader of her home. Just this year, he has begun to do that, much to her dismay. He wants to attend a different church.

My husband has become not only the spiritual leader, but a pastor. He went back to college and got his master's degree. It took him ten years and at the end of it, I wasn't so sure I wanted to be a pastor's wife. Be careful what you pray for.

Another woman is praying for her husband to give up smoking marijuana, another for a new job with better income, and another for her husband to stick to his diet.

My husband has grown into someone whom I admire and respect. He's even become romantic, something I thought I'd never see. He brings me flowers for no reason, praises my efforts at cooking and cleaning, and tells me I'm beautiful.

God is truly a miracle worker!

DON'T SUFFER ALONE

This fall my husband and I were guests on a call-in radio program. One of the callers was a woman whose husband was an alcoholic, and she feared he'd committed adultery. When we asked if she'd talked to anyone else, the answer was no. We were the first people she'd told about her problem. Don't suffer alone. Reach out to your friends, your church, or a counselor. If one counselor doesn't work, try another. Keep asking, seeking, and knocking on doors.

Develop friendships. Your relationship with your husband, no matter how wonderful, can't provide for all your needs. To be complete, we need friends. But how do you develop the kind of relationships that will last over the years?

When I was thirty-five I would have told you that I had no friends. Today I have many. What is the difference? I took on a new attitude. I stopped worrying about what others thought of me. Your world is full of women who are lonely and feel unloved. Become an ambassador for God and dispense his love.

I looked at other women and did for them what I was longing for someone to do for me. I reached out and called the women that I had always wanted to be my friends. I invited them out to lunch or coffee or to go shopping with me. I sent notes of encouragement.

I stopped assuming that everyone had friends but me. For years I lived next door to Robin. In my mind she was just about perfect. She was tall, blond, and thin. She made unique and beautiful crafts out of seemingly nothing and grew a garden that could have made the centerfold in *Sunset* magazine. I was scared of her. I couldn't imagine that she would find me interesting or fun to be with and so I kept her at arm's length. Recently I went to lunch with her. When I confessed this to her, she laughed because she said she thought of herself as a small-town girl and was afraid of me. I regret the years we wasted by being polite to one another. Now we are the best of friends.

Another key to friendships is respect. I never try to take up too much of anyone's time. Instead of worrying about whether or not they like me, I put me aside for a little while and find out about them. I ask questions; I look for areas where I can encourage them to be all that God intended; I try to be a good listener; I pray for them. I might not know what their needs are, but God does.

Close physical contact used to make me uncomfortable, but in recent years, I have learned the value of a hug. Not only am I giving one, I'm usually getting one in return. And they feel so good.

Telling people how much they mean to you is a powerful gift and one that is rarely given. Don't assume your friends know. We all need encouragement, no matter how good we look on the outside.

You are not alone in this world. There are many, many resources. Don't be afraid to reach out and ask people to help you.

If your husband is suffering from an addiction, whether it's chemical, sexual, or gambling, help is available. You need to reach out to groups such as Alanon to learn how you can help yourself and in the long run help your husband.

If you are experiencing physical abuse, then call the local help line, which I've listed again at the bottom of this page.* Also, most police departments now have domestic-violence advocates who can help you decide what to do about your situation. Even if your husband won't go for counseling, you go and get the help you need.

Don't go for counseling expecting the counselor to do all the work. He/she can't change you, only you can make the decisions necessary to make your life better.

When you begin to change, this might make your husband nervous. You have behaved a certain way for a long time, and when you begin to assert yourself and seek your own happiness it may be threatening to your husband. Expect it, but don't revert to old

---

* National Domestic Violence Hotline 1-800-799-7233.

behavior patterns. It's like a dance. At first you will step on his toes, but as he learns to adjust, you will get back in sync again.

No one truly knows happiness who has not suffered.
—HENRI AMIEL, *Journal*, 1992[10]

❧

We have been on a long journey. I hope what I've shared with you will be of some help. Divorce looks so easy, but it's only to be sought as a last resort. C. S. Lewis said:

Christians believe divorce is like a surgical operation. Some of us think that it's so violent that it shouldn't be done at all. Others think it should only be done as a desperate measure in extreme cases. We all agree that it's more like having both legs removed than dissolving a business partnership. Christians should not take the worldly view that it is a simple readjustment of partners, to be made whenever people feel they are no longer in love with one another or when either of them falls in love with someone else.[11]

Every time my family gathers for Christmas or birthdays or reunions, I'm thankful that I didn't choose divorce. When I look at the two young men whom we've raised, I'm filled with joy and pride. If I had left Larry, all that I am and enjoy today would not have been possible.

Yes, I've made some sacrifices, but I've also learned how much I get when I put others ahead of my own desires. My life is filled with wonderful people, and I've done things and gone places I would never have dreamed of before. Best of all, I have the respect of my children, my family, and my friends. One of our son's friends wrote to us from Annapolis and said we had been an example to him of how a Christian marriage works. He hoped someday he would have what we have. I can't imagine a better compliment than that.

I'll never forget the day I fell back in love with my husband. It had been seven years since that Marriage Encounter weekend when I recommitted myself to our marriage. I'd almost given up hope of ever feeling those "romantic" emotions again. We were on our way to Astoria, Oregon, for a weekend away. Things were strained between us and, to be honest, I wasn't even sure that I wanted to go. As we pulled onto the freeway, I knew something had to be said or we would both be miserable. I asked Larry to pull over. I told him how I was feeling, and then I asked if we could make this weekend a new beginning. We prayed together, and he pulled back onto the highway. I felt lighter than I had in weeks. We talked and laughed as we drove the hundred or so miles down the road. At one point we had to stop and take a small ferry across the Columbia River. I climbed out of the car and stood looking over the side of the boat at some eagles soaring overhead. Larry walked up behind me and put his arms around me. At that moment I was filled with a warmth that I thought I'd never feel again.

I feared it would not last past that weekend, but it did. God answered my cries and restored the years the locust had devoured (Joel 2:25).

I love my husband with a love that has been tested and made stronger. My life is filled with peace and joy, the kind that God promises us. None of this would've happened if I'd chosen divorce.

I pray that you don't either.

Notes

CHAPTER 2: IT'S FOR THE BEST

1. Diane Medved, *The Case against Divorce* (New York: Ivy Books, 1989) 194.
2. Genesis 2:24, NKJV.
3. Interlinear Bible (Seattle: PC Study Bible, 1993–97).
4. "Too Late for Prince Charming," *Newsweek,* 2 June 1986, 55.
5. Medved, *The Case against Divorce.*
6. Barbara Dafoe Whitehead, "Dan Quayle Was Right," *The Atlantic Monthly,* April 1993.
7. George Barna, *The Future of the American Family* (Chicago: Moody Press, 1993), 82.
8. Betty Holcomb, "Working Mothers on Trial," *Working Mother,* January 1995, 28.
9. Whitehead, "Dan Quayle Was Right."
10. Ibid.
11. "Child Support," *1995 Information Please Almanac* (New York: Houghton Mifflin Co., 1996) 435.
12. Whitehead, "Dan Quayle Was Right."
13. Patricia Chisholm, "Paying for the Children of Divorce," *Maclean's,* 10 January 1994, 36.
14. Lonnie K. Christiansen, "Broken Promises: Fighting for Child Support and Winning," *Family Circle,* 1 February 1996.
15. Whitehead, "Dan Quayle Was Right."
16. Anne Field, "Divorce Mediation and Other Cheap Ways to Split," *Cosmopolitan,* August 1995, 136.

17. "Divorce and Children: Guideline for Parents," *1996 Information Please Almanac* (New York: Houghton Mifflin Co., 1996), 435.
18. Whitehead, "Dan Quayle Was Right."
19. Ibid.
20. Joseph Adelson, "Splitting Up," *Commentary,* September 1996, 63.
21. Ben Gose, *The Chronicle of Higher Education,* 12 July 1996, A35.
22. Adelson, "Splitting Up."
23. Whitehead, "Dan Quayle Was Right."
24. Esther M. Berger, "Money Smart Divorce," *Booklist,* 15 February 1996, 971.
25. Adelson, "Splitting Up."
26. Whitehead, "Dan Quayle Was Right."
27. Ibid.
28. Katarzyna Wandycz, "Divorce Kills," *Forbes,* 25 October 1995, 240.
29. Excerpted from *True Serenity* by John Kirvan. Copyright 1995 by Quest Associates. Used with permission of Ave Maria Press, P.O. Box 428, Notre Dame, IN 46556.

CHAPTER 3: YOU DON'T KNOW HOW BAD THINGS ARE

1. Rebecca Davis and Susan Mesner, eds., *The Treasury of Religious and Spiritual Quotations* (Pleasantville, N.Y.: Reader's Digest, 1994), 302.
2. Matthew 19:8, *The Message.*
3. John 10:10.
4. Ed Wheat, M.D., and Gloria Okes Perkins, *Love Life for Every Married Couple* (New York: Harper Paperbacks, 1980), 275.
5. Matthew 7:1–5.
6. Psalm 91:11.
7. 1 John 1:8–9, NKJV.
8. Romans 8:4, *The Message.*
9. Romans 8:6, *The Message.*

CHAPTER 4: YOU DON'T KNOW MY HUSBAND

1. John Gray, Ph.D., *Men Are from Mars, Women Are from Venus* (New York: HarperCollins, 1992), 14.
2. Ibid., 15.
3. Patrick M. Morley, *What Husbands Wish Their Wives Knew about Men* (Grand Rapids, Mich.: Zondervan).
4. Ibid., 89.
5. Ibid., 50.

CHAPTER 5: I CAN'T FORGIVE OR FORGET

1. Matthew 12:34, italics mine.
2. 1 Peter 3:7; 1 John 1:9.
3. Isaiah 43:25, NKJV: "I, even I, am He who blots out your transgressions for My own sake; and I will not remember your sins."
4. Matthew 18:21–22, NKJV.

CHAPTER 6: I CAN'T CHANGE WHO I AM

1. George Christakis and Karen Miller-Kovach, "Maintenance of Weight Goal among Weight Watchers Lifetime Members," *Nutrition Today,* January/February 1996, 29.
2. Hebrews 4:13, NKJV.
3. Matthew 23:25, NKJV.
4. Matthew 5:21, 28; 1 John 3:15.
5. Matthew 11:28, NLT.
6. Mark 2:1–12.
7. Matthew 5:29.
8. Psalm 103:12, NKJV.

CHAPTER 7: I CAN'T CHANGE THE WAY I FEEL

1. Dr. James Dobson, *Emotions: Can You Trust Them?* (Ventura, Calif.: Regal, 1980), 10.
2. Psalm 69:1–3.
3. Taken from the hymn by J. H. Sammis and Daniel B. Towner, "Trust and Obey."

CHAPTER 8: I HAD SO MANY DREAMS

1. Reul Howe, *Sex and Religion Today,* ed. S. Doniger, 1953.
2. Ann Landers' column, *Eastside Journal,* 12 March 1998.
3. Romans 15:7.
4. Philippians 4:11–12.

CHAPTER 9: I DON'T LOVE HIM

1. Davis and Mesner, *The Treasury of Religious and Spiritual Quotations,* 308.
2. Kenneth Barker, gen. ed., *The NIV Study Bible: Study Notes* (Grand Rapids, Mich.: Zondervan, 1985), 11.
3. Romans 6:21–23, *The Message.*
4. Interlinear Bible.
5. Barker, *The NIV Study Bible: Study Notes*
6. Philippians 4:8, NKJV.
7. 2 Corinthians 10:5.
8. Barna, *The Future of the American Family,* 107.

CHAPTER 10: WE CAN'T TALK

1. James 3:7–10.
2. Matthew 5:33, *The Message.*
3. Howard Hendricks, *The Seven Laws of the Teacher* (Atlanta: Walk through the Bible Ministries, 1988), 42.
4. James 1:19, NKJV.

CHAPTER 11: I FEEL SO ANGRY

1. Galatians 5:22–23.
2. Exodus 11:8.
3. Acts 23:3.
4. Mark 3:4–5.
5. 1 John 3:15 and Matthew 5:22.
6. James 1:19–20, italics mine.

CHAPTER 12: I MARRIED THE WRONG MAN

1. Daniel J. Dolesh and Sherelynn Lehman, *Love Me, Love Me Not: How to Survive Infidelity* (New York: McGraw-Hill Company, 1985), 34.
2. Ibid., 35.
3. "Experts Give Advice on Avoiding Infidelity," *Jet,* 7 July 1997, 38.
4. Ester Davidowitz, "What's It Like to Be a Second Wife," *Redbook,* October 1994, 130.
5. Matthew 5:28, NKJV.
6. Shirley Glass and Hara Estroff Marano, "Shattered Vows," *Psychology Today,* July/August 1998, 34.
7. Ibid.
8. Ibid.
9. Dave Carder, *Torn Asunder* (Chicago: Moody Press, 1992), 97.
10. Romans 8:38–39.
11. Glass and Marano, "Shattered Vows."
12. Medved, *The Case against Divorce,* 131.
13. 1 John 1:9.
14. Philippians 4:8, NKJV.
15. 1 Corinthians 6:18–20, NKJV.
16. Matthew 5:29–30, NKJV.
17. 1 Peter 5:10.
18. Carder, *Torn Asunder,* 98.
19. Ibid., 96.
20. Ibid., 227.
21. "Secrets We Know about You," *Ladies Home Journal,* August 1986, 161.
22. Eric Weber and Steven S. Simring, M.D., *How to Win Back the One You Love* (New York: Macmillan Publishing, 1983), 112.
23. *Eastside Journal American,* Monday, 30 September 1996, D4.
24. Psalm 91:4.

CHAPTER 13: I DON'T WANT HIM TO TOUCH ME

1. Clifford and Joyce Penner, *The Gift of Sex* (Waco: Word, 1981), 85.
2. John Gray, Ph.D., *Mars and Venus in the Bedroom* (New York: HarperCollins, 1995), 2.

3. Dr. Deborah Newman, *Then God Created Woman* (Colorado Springs: Focus on the Family Publishing, 1997), 252.
4. "Sexuality, Contraception and Health," *Ladies Home Journal*, August 1986, 51.
5. Kristin Von Kreister, "The Healing Powers of Sex," *Reader's Digest*, June 1993, 17–20.
6. Ibid.
7. Ibid.
8. Ed Wheat, M.D., and Gaye Wheat, *Intended for Pleasure* (Grand Rapids, Mich.: Fleming H. Revell, 1981), 20.

CHAPTER 14: I DON'T FEEL LOVED

1. Matthew 11:30: "For my yoke is easy and my burden is light."
2. William A. (Billy) Sunday, sermon, New York, 1914, as quoted in Davis and Mesner, *The Treasury of Religious and Spiritual Quotations*, 276.
3. C. S. Lewis, *A Grief Observed*, as quoted in *The Quotable Lewis*, ed. Wayne Martindale and Jerry Root (Wheaton, Ill.: Tyndale House, 1989), 66–67.
4. Ephesians 3:17–19, *The Message*.
5. 1 Peter 1:8.
6. John 15:11.
7. Galatians 5:22.
8. Luke 6:31, 35, *The Message*.
9. Kirvan, *True Serenity*, 89–91.

CHAPTER 15: I JUST WANT TO BE HAPPY

1. Davis and Mesner, *The Treasury of Religious and Spiritual Quotations*, 222.
2. Norman Wright, *The Pillars of Marriage* (Ventura, Calif.: Regal Books, 1979), 31.
3. Susan J. Blumenthal and Deborah Pike, "Ten Things Every Woman Should Know about Depression," *Ladies Home Journal*, March 1996, 132.
4. Rona Maynard, "An Invisible Killer," *Chatelaine*, March 1997, 8.
5. Jean Endicott, Myrna M. Weissman, and Kimberly A. Yonkers, "What's Unique about Depression in Women?" *Patient Care*, 15 August 1996, 88.
6. Patricia Lopez Baden, "Beyond the Blues," *Better Homes and Gardens*, September 1995, 50.
7. Kim Pittaway, "If Drugs Cure Depression, Why Don't I Feel Better?" *Chatelaine*, March 1997, 46.
8. Baden, "Beyond the Blues."
9. "How to Tell If You're Not Getting Enough Sleep," *Jet*, 2 March 1998, 12.
10. Davis and Mesner, *The Treasury of Religious and Spiritual Quotations*, 231.
11. Paraphrased quote from *Mere Christianity*, *The Quotable Lewis*, Martindale and Root, 162.

Bibliography

Barna, George. *The Future of the American Family.* Chicago: Moody Press, 1993.

Carder, Dave. *Torn Asunder: Recovering from Extramarital Affairs.* Chicago: Moody Press, 1992.

Cook, Jerry. *Love, Acceptance and Forgiveness.* Ventura, Calif.: Regal Books, 1979.

Dobson, Dr. James. *Emotions: Can You Trust Them?* Ventura, Calif.: Regal Books, 1980.

Dolesh, Daniel J. and Sherelynn Lehman. *Love Me, Love Me Not: How to Survive Infidelity.* New York: McGraw-Hill, 1985.

Evans, Debra. *The Christian Woman's Guide to Sexuality.* Wheaton, Ill.: Crossway Books, 1997.

Gray, John, Ph.D. *Mars and Venus in the Bedroom.* New York: HarperCollins, 1995.

————. *Men Are from Mars, Women Are from Venus.* New York: HarperCollins, 1992.

Hendrix, Harville, Ph.D. *Getting the Love You Want.* New York: HarperPerennial, 1988.

Lerner, Harriet Goldhor, Ph.D. *The Dance of Anger.* New York: Harper & Row Publishers, 1985.

Medved, Diane. The Case Against Divorce. New York: Ivy Books, 1989.

Morley, Patrick M. *What Husbands Wish Their Wives Knew about Men.* Grand Rapids, Mich.: Zondervan, 1998.

Newman, Dr. Deborah. *Then God Created Woman.* Colorado Springs: Focus on the Family Publishing, 1997.

Northrup, Christiane, M.D. *Women's Bodies, Women's Wisdom.* New York: Bantam Books, 1998.

Omartian, Stormie. *Stormie.* Eugene, Oreg.: Harvest House, 1986.

Penner, Clifford and Joyce. *The Gift of Sex.* Waco: Word Books, 1981.

Tannen, Deborah, Ph.D. *You Just Don't Understand.* New York: Ballantine Books, 1990.

Weber, Eric and Steven S. Simring, M.D. *How to Win Back the One You Love.* New York: Macmillan Publishing, 1983.

Wheat, Ed, M.D., and Gaye Wheat. *Intended for Pleasure.* Grand Rapids, Mich.: Fleming H. Revell, 1981.

————, and Gloria Okes Perkins. *Love Life for Every Married Couple.* New York: HarperPaperbacks, 1980.

Whitehead, Barbara Dafoe. *The Divorce Culture.* New York: Alfred A. Knopf, 1997.

Whiteman, Thomas, Ph.D. *Innocent Victims.* Wayne, Pa.: Fresh Start, 1991.

Wright, H. Norman. *The Pillars of Marriage.* Ventura, Calif.: Regal Books, 1979.